150 best vegan muffin recipes

Camilla V. Saulsbury

Robert
ROSE

150 Best Vegan Muffin Recipes
Text copyright © 2012 Camilla V. Saulsbury
Photographs copyright © 2012 Robert Rose Inc.
Cover and text design copyright © 2012 Robert Rose Inc.

Some of the recipes in this book were previously published in *750 Best Muffin Recipes*,
published in 2010 by Robert Rose Inc.

For complete cataloguing information, see page 183.

Disclaimer
The recipes in this book have been carefully tested by our kitchen and our tasters. To the best
of our knowledge, they are safe and nutritious for ordinary use and users. For those people with
food or other allergies, or who have special food requirements or health issues, please read the
suggested contents of each recipe carefully and determine whether or not they may create a
problem for you. All recipes are used at the risk of the consumer.

We cannot be responsible for any hazards, loss or damage that may occur as a result of any
recipe use.

For those with special needs, allergies, requirements or health problems, in the event of
any doubt, please contact your medical adviser prior to the use of any recipe.

Design and Production: Daniella Zanchetta/PageWave Graphics Inc.
Editor: Sue Sumeraj
Recipe editor: Jennifer MacKenzie
Proofreader: Sheila Wawanash
Indexer: Gillian Watts
Photographer: Colin Erricson
Associate Photographer: Matt Johannsson
Food Stylist: Kathryn Robertson
Prop Stylist: Charlene Erricson

Cover image: Chocolate Chip Coffee Cake Muffins (page 110)

We acknowledge the financial support of the Government of Canada through the Book
Publishing Industry Development Program (BPIDP) for our publishing activities.

Published by Robert Rose Inc.
120 Eglinton Avenue East, Suite 800, Toronto, Ontario, Canada M4P 1E2
Tel: (416) 322-6552 Fax: (416) 322-6936
www.robertrose.ca

Printed and bound in Canada

1 2 3 4 5 6 7 8 9 MP 20 19 18 17 16 15 14 13 12

FSC
www.fsc.org
MIX
Paper from
responsible sources
FSC® C004191

Contents

Acknowledgments

To my publisher at Robert Rose, Bob Dees. I couldn't ask for more in a publisher.

To my amazing editors, Sue Sumeraj and Jennifer MacKenzie. I don't know how you make my hard word work feel like fun, but you do.

And to my family and friends, for making everything I do worth the effort.

Introduction

It's time for vegan muffins to take the limelight.

It was close to 20 years ago when I first came across a vegan muffin recipe in a favorite vegetarian magazine. "Vegan" had yet to become part of the popular culinary lexicon, so my reasons for trying the recipe had less to do with an interest in exploring a new way of baking than with the reality that I was out of milk and eggs. I was already in love with eating and making muffins, but I questioned whether muffins made without dairy and eggs could be anything more than an ersatz substitute for the "real" thing. But I was hungry, so I forged ahead.

Thank heavens I did, because the results were a delicious revelation. The fact that my humble batch of vegan muffins was absolutely gorgeous — a perfect rise and golden-brown bubble tops — got me excited, but the amazing taste and texture got me hooked. I am certain you will be too, once you give any of these muffins a try. Vegan muffins are the real deal, and the 150 muffins in this collection prove it with ease, innovation and plenty of good eating.

These are good times to venture into vegan muffin-making. Vegan baking is more popular than ever, and muffins — quick, simple and smashingly good — are the perfect choice when the urge to bake strikes. Moreover, what might have been considered elusive "vegan" ingredients a few years ago — non-dairy milk, soy yogurt, coconut oil and ground flax seeds — are now readily available at regular supermarkets.

Ever mindful of how vegan cooks are baking today, for this book I've created a modern collection of delicious muffin options. The chapter titles reflect my approach: My Top 20 Muffins, Breakfast Muffins, Coffeehouse Muffins, Lunch and Supper Muffins, and Global Muffins.

These are recipes you will want to make and enjoy again and again. The ingredients are simple and fresh, the flavors fantastic and the finished results beautiful. No esoteric baking equipment is required, though I have suggested a short list of tools that are handy to have around.

You'll find it hard to believe that breads so beautiful and delicious can be so quick and easy to make, but muffins prove that it's possible. Vegan muffins are a symbol of honest effort and are delicious anytime, anywhere. The fact that they are so easy to make is a huge plus for home cooks of all levels of experience these days. Thirty minutes in the kitchen pays dividends for several days. And in the end, what could be more satisfying than a basket brimming with warm-from-the-oven Blueberry Lemon Muffins (page 47), Pumpkin Spice Muffins (page 30) or Quinoa Multigrain Muffin (page 36)?

I hope you experience as much pleasure baking (and nibbling) your way through this cookbook as I did creating it; it was a labor of love, and I enjoyed every minute of it. Tasting is believing, so gather whisk and bowl and get baking. I know you'll savor every moment and morsel.

Muffin Mastery

A major part of the appeal of making muffins is their quick and straightforward preparation. The primary method can be broken down into a short list of simple steps:

1. **Preheat the oven.** Preheat to the temperature specified in the recipe.

2. **Prepare the muffin pan.** Line the cups with paper liners, or grease them with solid vegetable shortening, as specified in the recipe. To grease muffin cups, lightly but thoroughly coat the bottoms and sides, using a paper towel for ease of spreading (and to keep your fingers clean).

3. **Whisk the dry ingredients.** Whisking the dry ingredients distributes the baking powder, baking soda, salt and spices in the flour. If the leavening is not evenly distributed, the muffins may have a bitter taste.

4. **Whisk the wet ingredients.** Whisk the wet ingredients, such as milk, eggs, oil and melted butter, until thoroughly combined. Sugar is sometimes also whisked in with the wet ingredients.

5. **Combine the dry and wet ingredients.** Add the wet ingredients to the dry ingredients all at once. *Stir just until the dry ingredients are moistened and the batter is combined.* A few lumps are okay. Overmixing the batter develops the gluten in the flour, causing the baked muffins to have tunnels and a tough and/or gummy texture.

6. **Add any extra ingredients.** Gently stir or fold in any extra ingredients, such as berries or chocolate chips. As in step 5, the aim is to avoid overmixing.

7. **Fill the muffin pan.** Spoon the batter into the prepared muffin cups (or use a large, spring-loaded cookie or ice cream scoop). Place the muffin pan on the middle rack of the preheated oven.

8. **Bake and test for doneness.** Check for doneness using the method described in the recipe when the minimum baking time specified in the recipe has elapsed.

9. **Remove the muffins from the pan.** Let the muffins cool in the pan for a few minutes, as specified in the recipe, then remove to a wire rack to cool further. If you leave the muffins in the pan to cool, the bottoms will get soggy.

Creamed Muffins

A small number of recipes in this collection direct you to cream the vegan margarine and sugar with an electric mixer before adding the other wet ingredients. As with the primary method above, take special care in combining the dry ingredients with the creamed mixture to avoid overmixing.

Transforming Standard Muffins into Loaves, Mini Muffins and Jumbo Muffins

All of the recipes in this collection are written for use with a standard-size muffin pan. But refashioning any of the recipes into loaves, mini muffins or jumbo muffins is easy. Preheat the oven and prepare the batter as specified in the recipe, then follow the guidelines below for the desired type of pan or pan.

Loaves

Grease and flour a light-colored metal loaf pan or pans to prevent the loaf from sticking (due to the longer bake time required by a loaf). Spread the batter in the prepared pan, smoothing the top with a rubber spatula so that the loaf rises and browns evenly during baking. Place the pan in the preheated oven and bake for 5 to 20 minutes longer than the specified muffin baking time (the timing will depend on what size loaf pan you use). Test for doneness in the same manner as described for testing muffins. Let the loaf cool in the pan for 10 minutes. Run a butter knife around the sides of the loaf and unmold. Transfer the loaf, upright, to a wire rack to cool further.

Mini Muffins

Prepare the mini muffin pan as specified for the standard muffin pan in the recipe (i.e., greased or lined with paper liners). In general, a recipe with a yield of 12 standard muffins will yield 24 mini muffins. Fill

the prepared muffin pans, then place in the oven. Reduce the baking time by 5 to 15 minutes, checking for doneness at the earliest time. Test for doneness in the same manner as described for testing the standard-size muffins. Let cool in the pan for the same amount of time as specified in the standard muffin recipe, then remove to a wire rack to cool further.

Jumbo Muffins

Prepare the jumbo muffin pan as specified for the standard muffin pan in the recipe (i.e., greased or lined with paper liners). In general, a recipe with a yield of 12 standard muffins will yield 6 jumbo muffins. Fill the prepared muffin pans, then place in the oven. Increase the baking time by 5 to 15 minutes, checking for doneness at the earliest time. Test for doneness in the same manner as described for testing the standard-size muffins. Let cool in the pan for the same amount of time as specified in the standard muffin recipe, then remove to a wire rack to cool further.

Measuring Ingredients

Television baking shows give the illusion that baking is a freestyle event — a pinch of this here, a dash of that there, and voila! Perfect cookies, cakes and muffins. In reality, baking is much more like a chemistry experiment (albeit a delicious one) than a magic show. Accurate measurements are essential for creating the perfect balance of flour, liquids, leaveners and fats, and achieving consistent results time and again. Too much flour makes muffins taste dry and flavorless, too little baking powder makes them flat, and an excess of salt renders them inedible. So take both time and care as you measure; the success of your muffins depends on it.

Measuring Dry Ingredients

When measuring a dry ingredient, such as flour, cocoa powder, sugar, spices or salt, spoon it into the appropriate-size dry measuring cup or measuring spoon, heaping it up over the top. Slide a straight-edged utensil, such as a knife, across the top to level off the extra. Be careful not to shake or tap the cup or spoon to settle the ingredient, or you will have more than you need.

Measuring Moist Ingredients

Moist ingredients, such as brown sugar, coconut and dried fruit, must be firmly packed in a measuring cup or spoon to be measured accurately. Use a dry measuring cup for these ingredients. Fill the measuring cup to slightly overflowing, then pack down the ingredient firmly with the back of a spoon. Add more of the ingredient and pack down again until the cup is full and even with the top of the measure.

Measuring Liquid Ingredients

Use a clear plastic or glass measuring cup or container with lines up the sides to measure liquid ingredients. Set the container on the counter and pour the liquid to the appropriate mark. Lower your head to read the measurement at eye level.

Ingredients for Vegan Muffins

Vegan muffins are baking favorites because, in addition to their ease of preparation and quick baking time, the essential ingredients are familiar and commonly stocked in most home pantries. Do you have all-purpose flour, baking powder, salt, sugar, oil and non-dairy milk? Then you have what you need to make a basic vegan muffin that can be dressed up or down with an endless array of mix-ins, from fruit (fresh or dried) to nuts to chocolate. Craving a whole-grain muffin? Swap in some whole wheat flour for some or all of the all-purpose flour. Cutting back on refined sugar? Use an alternative sweetener such as agave nectar, turbinado sugar, brown rice syrup, molasses or maple syrup in place of the granulated sugar. What follows are the key ingredients to keep on hand for a wealth of vegan muffin recipes.

Flours, Grains and Nuts

All-Purpose Flour

Made from a blend of high-gluten hard wheat and low-gluten soft wheat, all-purpose flour is a fine-textured flour milled from the inner part of the wheat kernel and contains neither the germ nor the bran. All-purpose flour comes either bleached or unbleached; they can be used interchangeably.

Replacing All-Purpose Flour with Whole Wheat Flour

Generally, you can replace white flour with whole wheat flour of the same type (bread for bread, all-purpose for all-purpose), substituting one for one. However, products made with whole wheat flour will usually be denser, because the flakes of bran in whole wheat flour can weaken the gluten structure of baked goods. A good rule of thumb for muffins is to substitute no more than half the all-purpose flour with whole wheat flour. And since whole wheat flour absorbs more liquid than all-purpose flour, it is a good idea to increase the total amount of liquid slightly.

Whole Wheat Pastry Flour

A fine-textured, soft wheat flour that includes the wheat germ, whole wheat pastry flour can be used interchangeably with all-purpose flour in most recipes. In many recipes in this book, I've used it in combination with all-purpose flour, but feel free to up the proportion of whole wheat pastry flour to replace more or all of the all-purpose flour.

It is extremely important not to substitute regular whole wheat flour for the whole wheat pastry flour; the results will be coarse, leaden and possibly inedible.

You can find whole wheat pastry flour at well-stocked supermarkets and at natural food stores. Store it in a sealable plastic bag in the refrigerator.

Whole Wheat Flour

Whole wheat flour is milled from hard red wheat; it has a fuller flavor and is far more nutritious than all-purpose flour because it contains the wheat bran and sometimes the germ. Because of its higher fat content, it should be stored in the refrigerator to prevent rancidity.

Measure Flour with the Stir, Spoon and Sweep Method.

First, stir the flour in the canister or storage container. When flour is stirred, air is added to it, which lightens and decompacts it. Next, lightly spoon the ingredient into a dry measuring cup. Holding the cup over the flour container, sweep off the excess at the top with a long, flat implement, such as a spatula or knife. This method will ensure that the correct amount of flour is added to the batter.

Cornmeal

Cornmeal is simply ground dried corn kernels. There are two methods of grinding. The first is the modern method, in which milling is done by huge steel rollers, which remove the husk and germ almost entirely; this creates the most common variety of cornmeal found in supermarkets. The second is the stone-ground method, in which some of the hull and germ of the corn is retained; this type of cornmeal is available at health food stores and in the health food sections of most supermarkets. The two varieties can be used interchangeably in most of the recipes in this collection, but I recommend sticking with the stone-ground variety where specified, as it has a much deeper corn flavor and is far more nutritious.

Rolled Oats

Two types of rolled oats are called for in these recipes: large-flake (old-fashioned) rolled oats are oat groats (hulled and cleaned whole oats) that have been steamed and flattened with huge rollers; quick-cooking rolled oats are groats that have been cut into several pieces before being steamed and rolled into thinner flakes. For the best results, it is important to use the type of rolled oats specified in the recipe.

Ground Flax Seeds (Flaxseed Meal)

Flax seeds are highly nutritious, tiny seeds from the flax plant. They have gained tremendous popularity in recent years thanks to their high levels of omega-3 fatty acids. But to reap the most benefits from the seeds, you must grind them into meal. Look for packages of ready-ground flax seeds, which may be labeled "flaxseed meal," or grind whole flax seeds in a spice or coffee grinder to a very fine meal. The meal adds a warm, nutty flavor to a wide range of muffins throughout the collection, and is also used as an egg substitute in many of the recipes. Store ground flax seeds in an airtight bag in the refrigerator for 4 to 5 months, or in the freezer for up to 8 months.

Nuts

I've used a wide variety of nuts in this collection, including walnuts, pecans, almonds, pine nuts and pistachios. Many of the recipes call for the nuts to be toasted before they are added to the muffin batter. Toasting nuts deepens their flavor and makes them crisp. To toast nuts, spread the amount needed for the recipe on a rimmed baking sheet. Bake in a preheated 350°F (180°C) oven for 8 to 10 minutes or until golden and fragrant. Alternatively, toast the nuts in a dry skillet over low heat, stirring constantly, for 2 to 4 minutes or until golden and fragrant.

Leaveners

Baking Powder

Baking powder is a chemical leavening agent made from a blend of alkali (sodium bicarbonate, known commonly as baking soda) and acid (most commonly calcium acid phosphate, sodium aluminum sulfate or cream of tartar), plus some form of starch to absorb any moisture so a reaction does not take place until a liquid is added to the batter. When baking powder is combined with a liquid, a chemical reaction produces carbon dioxide, which is trapped in tiny air pockets in the baked good's dough or batter. Heat releases additional carbon dioxide and expands the trapped gas and air to create steam. The pressure expands the air pockets, thus expanding the food.

All of the recipes in this collection calling for baking powder were tested using double-acting baking powder. It is the most common variety, and is readily available in supermarkets.

If you find yourself without baking powder as you prepare to bake, use this simple substitution: for every 1 tsp (5 mL) commercial baking powder, use a combination of $\frac{1}{4}$ tsp (1 mL) baking soda, $\frac{1}{2}$ tsp (2 mL) cream of tartar and $\frac{1}{4}$ tsp (1 mL) cornstarch.

Testing the Potency of Baking Powder

Baking powder loses its potency over time. To test your supply before using it in a recipe, pour $\frac{1}{3}$ cup (75 mL) hot water over $\frac{1}{2}$ tsp (2 mL) baking powder in a cup. The mixture should bubble vigorously. If it does not, toss the baking powder out and purchase a new container.

Avoid Too Much Leavening

When your vegan muffins turn out dense and heavy, you might think the solution is simple: add more baking powder to the recipe. But the opposite is often true: the problem may be *too much* baking powder or baking soda. When muffin batter has too much of either of these chemical leaveners, the gas bubbles in the batter get big, float to the top and then pop. The leavening in the batter is gone and the muffins are flat and dense. So, for best results, measure leaveners precisely.

Baking Soda

Baking soda is a chemical leavener consisting of bicarbonate of soda. It is alkaline in nature and, when combined with an acidic ingredient such as buttermilk, yogurt, sour cream, citrus juice, honey or molasses, it creates carbon dioxide bubbles, giving baked goods a dramatic rise.

Baking soda is approximately four times as strong as baking powder, which is why it is typically used in small quantities. Moreover, too much baking soda will add a soapy taste and produce muffins with large holes and a coarse texture. Baking soda starts to react and release carbon dioxide gas the moment it combines with liquid in a recipe, so make sure to finish the batter and send it to the oven immediately.

Testing the Potency of Baking Soda

There is no accurate way to test the potency of baking soda. As a general rule, though, replace the box every 6 months for optimal freshness. Write the date the box was opened on the front, for an easy reminder.

Sweeteners

Vegan Granulated Sugar

Granulated sugar (also called white sugar) is refined cane or beet sugar, and is the most common sweetener used in this book. Once opened, store granulated sugar in an airtight container in a cool, dry place.

Vegan Brown Sugar

Brown sugar is granulated sugar with some molasses added to it. The molasses gives the brown sugar a soft texture. Light brown sugar (also known as golden yellow sugar) has less molasses and a more delicate flavor than dark brown sugar.

Once opened, store brown sugar in an airtight container or a sealable plastic food bag, to prevent clumping.

Vegan Confectioners' (Icing) Sugar

Confectioners' (icing) sugar (also called powdered sugar) is granulated sugar that has been ground to a fine powder. Cornstarch is added to prevent the sugar from clumping together. It is used in recipes where regular sugar would be too grainy.

Turbinado Sugar

Turbinado sugar is raw sugar that has been steam-cleaned. The coarse crystals are blond in color and have a delicate molasses flavor. They are typically used for decoration and texture atop baked goods. Turbinado sugar is vegan; it does not go through a bone char filter because the brown color is desirable.

Evaporated Cane Juice

Evaporated cane juice is a less refined version of granulated sugar. It is always a vegan product because it does not undergo a bone char filtering process. Rather, it is made by extracting, clarifying, evaporating and crystallizing sugar cane juice. The result is a blond-colored, natural sugar that can be used as a one-for-one replacement for granulated sugar. Several companies also produce a powdered sugar made from evaporated cane juice that can be used as a one-for-one replacement for confectioners' (icing) sugar.

Refined Sugars: Are They Vegan?

Refined sugars — granulated (white) sugar, brown sugar and confectioners' (icing) sugar — do not contain any animal products, so, by an ingredients-based definition, refined sugars are vegan. However, some refined sugar is processed with bone char, derived from the sun-bleached bones of cattle. The bone is heated to an extremely high temperature, which results in a physical change in its composition. The bone becomes pure carbon before it is used in the sugar refining process; therefore, refined sugar does not contain any bone particles. The charcoal is used to remove color, impurities and minerals from sugar. The charcoal is not "in" the sugar, but is used in the process as a filter. By a process-based definition, refined sugar may not be considered vegan.

While the bone char filter is used by some large sugar companies, it is not used to produce all refined sugar. The two major types of refined sugar produced in the North America are beet sugar and cane sugar; they are identically labeled save for the ingredients list, are nutritionally equivalent and can be used interchangeably in recipes. Beet sugar refineries never use a bone char filter in processing because this type of sugar does not require an extensive procedure to remove color. But not all cane sugar refineries use the bone char filter process either.

Here's the bottom line when you're selecting refined sugars:

1. If you follow an ingredients-based definition of veganism, any variety of refined sugar is acceptable.
2. If you follow a process-based definition of veganism, opt for either beet sugar products or cane sugar products that do not use the bone char filter process.

Alternatively, you can use unrefined sugars in place of refined sugars. Specifically, use evaporated cane juice in place of granulated sugar and Sucanat in place of brown sugar.

Sucanat

Sucanat stands for SU(gar) CA(ne) NAT(ural). It is a type of evaporated cane juice made from the whole sugar cane, and it is always vegan. Sucanat is produced by extracting juice from the sugar cane and boiling it in a large vat to remove the water. But unlike other evaporated cane juices, the sweet syrup that remains is not spun and crystallized in the vat. Instead, it's hand-paddled to cool it and dry it. This process creates dry granules that retain all of the sugar cane's molasses, which translates into a deep flavor and dark brown color. Sucanat can be used as a one-for-one replacement for refined brown sugar.

Maple Syrup

Maple syrup is a thick liquid sweetener made by boiling the sap from maple trees. It has a strong, pure maple flavor. Maple-flavored pancake syrup is just corn syrup with coloring and artificial maple flavoring added, and it is not recommended as a substitute for pure maple syrup. Unopened containers of maple syrup may be stored at room temperature. After opening, store maple syrup in the refrigerator to protect against mold. Maple syrup will keep indefinitely when stored properly.

Molasses

Molasses is made from the juice of sugar cane or sugar beets, which is boiled until a syrupy mixture remains. The recipes in this collection were tested using dark (cooking) molasses, but you can substitute light (fancy) molasses if you prefer. Blackstrap molasses is thick and very dark, and it has a bitter flavor; it is not recommended for the recipes in this collection. Unopened containers of molasses may be stored at room temperature. After opening, store molasses in the refrigerator to protect against mold. Molasses will keep indefinitely when stored properly.

Molasses Is Always Vegan

Molasses made for human consumption does not undergo any type of char filter, because the deep brown color is a desirable aspect of the product.

Agave Nectar

Agave nectar (or agave syrup) is a plant-based sweetener derived from the agave cactus, native to Mexico. Used for centuries to make tequila, agave juice produces a light golden syrup.

Using agave nectar as a sweetener can help keep muffins moist. You can substitute agave nectar for sugar in muffin recipes, but a few adjustments are necessary. Agave nectar is sweeter than granulated sugar, so for every 1 cup (250 mL) of sugar, use $2/3$ cup (150 mL) agave nectar. Because agave nectar is up to 20% water, reduce the amount of liquid in the recipe by $1/4$ cup (60 mL) for each cup (250 mL) of agave nectar used. Add $1/2$ tsp (2 mL) baking soda for each cup (250 mL) of agave nectar used. Reduce the oven temperature by 25°F (10°C), as agave nectar browns baking goods more than sugar.

Brown Rice Syrup

Brown rice syrup is made from brown rice that has been soaked, sprouted and cooked with an enzyme that breaks the starches into maltose. Brown rice syrup has a light, mild flavor and a similar appearance to honey, though it is less sweet. An equal amount of brown rice syrup can be substituted for honey or maple syrup.

Why Honey Is Not Considered Vegan

Insects are animals, so insect products such as honey are not traditionally considered vegan. Some vegans, however, do use honey, contending that its production causes no more distress for insects than the production and harvest of most fruits and vegetables (the harvesting and transportation of fruits and vegetables involves many "collateral" insect deaths). Nevertheless, when cooking or baking for vegans, it's best to be on the safe side and exclude honey.

Fats and Oils

Vegetable Oil

"Vegetable oil" is a generic term used to describe any neutral, plant-based oil that is liquid at room temperature. You can use a vegetable oil blend, canola oil, light olive oil, grapeseed oil, safflower oil, sunflower oil, peanut oil or corn oil.

Olive Oil

Olive oil is a monounsaturated oil that is prized for a wide range of cooking preparations, including soups. Plain olive oil (the products are simply labeled "olive oil") contains a combination of refined olive oil and virgin or extra virgin oil. It has a mild flavor and is significantly less expensive than extra virgin olive oil. Extra virgin olive oil is the cold-pressed result of the first pressing of the olives and is considered the finest and fruitiest of the olive oils.

Unrefined Virgin Coconut Oil

Virgin coconut oil is a delicious option for adding richness to vegan muffins. It is semi-solid at room temperature and must be melted slowly, over low heat, to avoid burning it.

Vegan Margarine

Margarine is used for a number of recipes in this collection. Read the label closely to ensure that the product is 100% vegan, as some margarines include milk solids.

Avoid Margarine Spreads

The recipes in this collection that call for margarine were tested with Earth Balance Vegan Buttery Sticks. Margarine spreads — in tub or stick form — should not be used. In order to be "spreadable," these products contain a much higher percentage of water than margarine sticks. Using spreads instead of sticks will alter the liquid and fat combination of the recipe, leading to either unsatisfactory or downright disastrous results. For best results, choose vegan margarine sticks that have at least an 80% fat content.

Non-Dairy Milks, Yogurt and Cream Cheese

Non-dairy milks are essential for vegans, as well as for those who are lactose-intolerant or have dairy allergies. The variety and availability of non-dairy milks is greater than ever, and you cannot beat their shelf-stable convenience. Following are some of the varieties to consider.

Stick with Plain and Unsweetened

Non-dairy milks — soy, almond, rice and hemp — are available sweetened or unsweetened in a wide variety of flavors and fat percentages. Unless otherwise specified, always use plain, unsweetened, regular (not reduced-fat) non-dairy milk for the recipes in this collection.

Soy Milk

Soy milk is made by grinding soybeans, mixing in water and cooking. Finally, the liquid is pressed from the solids and then filtered.

Almond Milk

Almond milk is made from almonds, water, sea salt and typically a small amount of sweetener. It works particularly well as a substitute for dairy milk in baked good recipes.

Rice Milk

Rice milk is made from brown rice, water, sea salt and typically a small amount of oil. It is a very light, sweet beverage that can replace dairy milk in most recipes.

Hemp Milk

Hemp milk is a thick, rich milk made from hemp seeds, water and a touch of brown rice syrup. It is rich in healthy omega-3 fatty acids, protein and essential vitamins and minerals. It can be used in a broad range of sweet and savory dishes.

Coconut Milk

Typically available canned or in Tetra Paks, coconut milk adds instant exotic flair and richness to muffins. It is readily available and very affordable at supermarkets.

Soy Yogurt

Soy yogurt is made by adding live cultures to a soy milk base. Like dairy yogurt, it is acidic and tenderizes baked goods.

Non-Dairy Cream Cheese

Non-dairy cream cheese (such as Tofutti Better Than Cream Cheese) is similar in both taste and texture to dairy cream cheese. It is typically packaged in tubs, and while it does not need to be softened before use (it has a spreadable consistency), it works best in baking recipes when first brought to room temperature.

Vegan Chocolate and Cocoa Powder

The variety of vegan chocolate options has never been better, and identifying what is and isn't vegan is fairly simple: choose a chocolate with 50% to 70% cocoa solids in the ingredient list and no dairy or milk solids. If you have any doubts, a quick call to the customer service number on the package can confirm the ingredients. Also avoid vegetable fat and artificial flavors. Look for cocoa butter instead. A high percentage of sugar is an indicator of lower quality.

Good chocolate should have an even color, but if chocolate develops a white or gray sheen, it is not spoiled; rather, it has "bloomed," meaning that it got warm enough for the cocoa butter's crystalline bonds to break and reform in an irregular pattern (fat bloom) or that water has condensed on the chocolate's surface (sugar bloom). Bloom does not damage the chocolate for cooking purposes but may make it grainy and less palatable for eating plain.

Bittersweet Baking Chocolate

Bittersweet chocolate is the variety called for most in this collection of recipes. At its most basic, chocolate is made up of cocoa butter and cocoa powder — which together are called cacao liquor and determine cacao content — along with sugar. As cacao content goes up, sugar content goes down. Bittersweet chocolate has a high percentage of cacao (anywhere from 35% to 99%), a more assertive chocolate flavor and a lower percentage of sugar.

Vegan Chocolate Chips

Chocolate chips are small chunks of chocolate that are typically sold in a round, flat-bottomed teardrop shape. They are available in numerous sizes, from large to miniature, but are usually around $\frac{1}{2}$ inch (1 cm) in diameter. Look for varieties without any milk solids or other dairy products in the ingredient list.

Cocoa Powder

Cocoa powder is naturally vegan. My preference is natural cocoa powder, rather than Dutch process, for the recipes in this collection. Natural cocoa powder has a deep, true chocolate flavor. The packaging should state whether it is Dutch process or not, but you can also tell the difference by sight: if it is dark to almost black, it is Dutch process; natural cocoa powder is much lighter and is typically brownish-red in color.

Natural vs. Dutch Process Cocoa

Dutch process cocoa has been treated with alkali, which increases the pH of the cocoa powder and mellows sharp flavors. I find that natural cocoa powder produces muffins with a more complex chocolate profile.

However, you are more than welcome to substitute an equal amount of Dutch process cocoa for any and all of the recipes in this collection if it suits your preference. Some baking books caution against substituting one type of cocoa for another: the success of a baking recipe depends on a specific pH balance. I have put the substitution to the test in many baking recipes, from muffins to cakes to cookies. I found no difference in any of the recipes regardless of which type of cocoa powder I used. Nevertheless, if you use a Dutch process cocoa powder, I recommend choosing a high-quality one.

Flavorings

Salt

Unless otherwise specified, the recipes in this collection were tested with ordinary table salt. Salt connoisseurs often prefer to use kosher salt, which is all-natural and additive-free; you are welcome to substitute it (the fine kosher salt, not the coarse) for the table salt.

Black Pepper

Black pepper is made by grinding black peppercorns, which have been picked when the berry is not quite ripe, then dried until it shrivels and the skin turns dark brown to black. Black pepper has a strong, slightly hot flavor, with a hint of sweetness.

Spices

All of the recipes in this collection use ground spices (as opposed to whole spices). With ground spices, freshness is everything. To determine whether a ground spice is fresh, open the container and sniff. A strong fragrance means the spice is still acceptable for use.

Checking Spices for Freshness

Ensuring that your ground spices are fresh is as simple as following these four easy steps:

- Check the expiration date on the bottle. Ideally, it should be at least 6 months away.
- Throw away old opened spices. Even if the expiration date is still more than 6 months away, discard spices that have been open for longer than 6 months. Place a small sticker on the bottom of the container and mark the date it was opened, to help you remember.
- Store spices properly. A decorative display of glass bottles above the stove or by the window may look beautiful, but spices will stay fresh much longer if stored in airtight, opaque containers in a cool, dark cabinet.
- Replenish spices at health food and whole food stores. An inexpensive way to ensure fresh spices is to buy them in bulk at these stores. The difference in cost is substantial, allowing for routine replacement of spices.

Vanilla Extract

Vanilla extract adds a sweet, fragrant flavor to countless varieties of muffins; it is particularly good for enhancing the flavors of chocolate and fresh fruit. It is produced by combining an extraction from dried vanilla beans with an alcohol and water mixture. It is then aged for several months. The three most common types of vanilla beans used to make vanilla extract are Bourbon-Madagascar, Mexican and Tahitian.

Almond Extract

Almond extract is a flavoring manufactured by combining bitter almond oil with ethyl alcohol. It is used in much the same way as vanilla extract. Almond extract has a highly concentrated, intense flavor, so measure with care.

Citrus Zest

Zest is the name for the colored outer layer of citrus peel. The oils in zest are intense in flavor. Use a zester, a Microplane-style grater or the small holes of a box grater to grate zest. Avoid grating the white layer (pith) just below the zest; it is very bitter.

Instant Espresso Powder

Stronger than regular coffee powder, a small amount of espresso powder can dramatically flavor a wide variety of muffin batters. It is available where coffee is shelved in most supermarkets and at specialty stores.

The Dirty Dozen and the Clean Fifteen

The Environmental Working Group (EWG), a non-profit organization, created the *Shoppers Guide to Pesticides in Produce*. The 2011 edition of the guide is based on the results of 51,000 tests for pesticides on produce, conducted from 2000 to 2009 by the U.S. Department of Agriculture and the federal Food and Drug Administration. It's important to note that the EWG states that almost all of the tests were performed on produce that had been rinsed or peeled. For more information, visit www.ewg.org.

The Dirty Dozen

Here are the top 12 most pesticide-contaminated fruits and vegetables in America. When shopping for these items, buy organic whenever possible.

1. Apples
2. Celery
3. Strawberries
4. Peaches
5. Spinach
6. Nectarines (imported)
7. Grapes (imported)
8. Bell peppers
9. Potatoes
10. Blueberries
11. Lettuce
12. Kale/collard greens

The Clean Fifteen

These fruits and vegetables are the least contaminated by pesticides, so it's not as crucial to buy organic.

1. Onions
2. Sweet corn
3. Pineapples
4. Avocados
5. Asparagus
6. Sweet peas
7. Mangos
8. Eggplants
9. Cantaloupe (domestic)
10. Kiwifruit
11. Cabbage
12. Watermelon
13. Sweet potatoes
14. Grapefruit
15. Mushrooms

Equipment

Great muffins require minimal equipment. Here is a short list of what you'll need:

Essential Checklist

- Standard muffin pans: cups typically hold $\frac{1}{2}$ cup (125 mL)
- Mixing bowls
- 1-cup (250 mL) and 2-cup (500 mL) liquid measuring cups (preferably clear glass or plastic)
- Dry measuring cups in graduated sizes: $\frac{1}{4}$ cup (60 mL), $\frac{1}{3}$ cup (75 mL), $\frac{1}{2}$ cup (125 mL) and 1 cup (250 mL)
- Measuring spoons in graduated sizes
- Wire whisk
- Kitchen/chef's knife
- Cutting boards
- Wooden spoons
- Silicone or rubber spatulas
- Electric blender (standard upright or handheld immersion style)
- Kitchen timer
- Box grater/shredder
- Oven mitts or holders
- Zester or Microplane-style grater (for removing zest from citrus fruits)
- Wooden toothpicks (for testing doneness of muffins)

Extras

- Spring-loaded cookie or ice cream scoop, large size (typically 3 tbsp/45 mL)
- Mini muffin pans: cups typically hold $\frac{1}{4}$ cup (60 mL)
- Jumbo muffin pans: cups typically hold $\frac{3}{4}$ cup (175 mL)
- Light-colored metal loaf pans:
  Large: 9 by 5 by 3 inches (23 by 12.5 by 7.5 cm), 8-cup (2 L) capacity
  Medium: $8\frac{1}{2}$ by $4\frac{1}{2}$ by $2\frac{1}{2}$ inches (21 by 11 by 6 cm), 6-cup (1.5 L) capacity
  Small: 6 by 3 by 2 inches (15 by 7.5 by 5 cm), 2-cup (500 mL) capacity

My Top 20 Muffins

Best Basic Muffins

Makes 12 muffins

I call these "basic" muffins, yet they are everything but that. They are pure comfort, without being remotely stodgy. Use them as a template for creating countless variations of your own design, adding spices, dried fruits, nuts, seeds, herbs, extract — you name it. Or keep them simple and eat one straight up, with a cup of hot cocoa or tea.

Tip: When baking a batch of muffins that does not use all the cups of a muffin pan, fill the empty cups halfway with water. This prevents the pan from buckling and the empty cups from scorching. The extra humidity from the water also contributes to the moisture of the muffins.

- Preheat oven to 400°F (200°C)
- 12-cup muffin pan, greased

2 cups	all-purpose flour	500 mL
2 tsp	baking powder	10 mL
1/2 tsp	baking soda	2 mL
1/2 tsp	salt	2 mL
2/3 cup	vegan granulated sugar or evaporated cane juice	150 mL
3/4 cup	plain non-dairy milk (soy, almond, rice, hemp)	175 mL
3/4 cup	vanilla-flavored soy yogurt	175 mL
1/3 cup	vegetable oil	75 mL
1 tsp	vanilla extract	5 mL

1. In a large bowl, whisk together flour, baking powder, baking soda and salt.

2. In a medium bowl, whisk together sugar, milk, yogurt, oil and vanilla until well blended.

3. Add the yogurt mixture to the flour mixture and stir until just blended.

4. Divide batter equally among prepared muffin cups.

5. Bake in preheated oven for 18 to 22 minutes or until tops are golden brown and a toothpick inserted in the center comes out clean. Let cool in pan on a wire rack for 3 minutes, then transfer to the rack to cool.

Fresh Apple Muffins

Makes 18 muffins

Apple pie meets everyone's favorite morning bread. In other words, this is like an apple pie in your hand.

Tip: Place a slightly damp dish towel or moist paper towel underneath your cutting board to prevent skidding and to absorb any juices from fruits or vegetables that may run off from your food.

- Preheat oven to 375°F (190°C)
- Blender
- Two 12-cup muffin pans, 18 cups greased

1 cup	all-purpose flour	250 mL
½ cup	whole wheat flour	125 mL
1 tsp	ground cinnamon	5 mL
1 tsp	baking powder	5 mL
½ tsp	baking soda	2 mL
½ tsp	salt	2 mL
¼ tsp	ground nutmeg	1 mL
3 tbsp	ground flax seeds	45 mL
⅓ cup	packed vegan light brown sugar or Sucanat	75 mL
⅓ cup	vegan granulated sugar or evaporated cane juice	75 mL
½ cup	vegetable oil	125 mL
1½ tsp	vanilla extract	7 mL
1½ cups	chopped peeled apples	375 mL

1. In a large bowl, whisk together all-purpose flour, whole wheat flour, cinnamon, baking powder, baking soda, salt and nutmeg.

2. In blender, process flax seeds and ½ cup (125 mL) water for 1 minute or until thickened and frothy. Add brown sugar, granulated sugar, oil and vanilla; process for 2 minutes or until well blended and frothy.

3. Add the flax seed mixture to the flour mixture and stir until just blended. Gently fold in apples.

4. Divide batter equally among prepared muffin cups.

5. Bake in preheated oven for 25 to 28 minutes or until tops are golden brown and a toothpick inserted in the center comes out clean. Let cool in pans on a wire rack for 5 minutes, then transfer to the rack to cool.

Applesauce Raisin Muffins

Makes 12 muffins

Whether you use store-bought applesauce or make your own, this pure comfort muffin will make it hard to stop after just one.

Tip: To maintain the oven temperature as much as possible during baking, don't open the oven door unless absolutely necessary. Take advantage of the oven light, peer through the window and wait until the minimum baking time to open the door.

- Preheat oven to 400°F (200°C)
- 12-cup muffin pan, greased

2 cups	all-purpose flour	500 mL
2 tsp	baking powder	10 mL
1 tsp	ground cinnamon	5 mL
1/2 tsp	ground allspice	2 mL
1/2 tsp	baking soda	2 mL
1/2 tsp	salt	2 mL
2/3 cup	vegan granulated sugar or evaporated cane juice	150 mL
1 1/3 cups	unsweetened applesauce	325 mL
1/3 cup	vegetable oil	75 mL
1 tsp	vanilla extract	5 mL
1/2 cup	raisins	125 mL

1. In a large bowl, whisk together flour, baking powder, cinnamon, allspice, baking soda and salt.

2. In a medium bowl, whisk together sugar, applesauce, oil and vanilla until well blended.

3. Add the applesauce mixture to the flour mixture and stir until just blended. Gently fold in raisins.

4. Divide batter equally among prepared muffin cups.

5. Bake in preheated oven for 25 to 28 minutes or until tops are golden brown and a toothpick inserted in the center comes out clean. Let cool in pan on a wire rack for 5 minutes, then transfer to the rack to cool.

Berry Jam Muffins

Makes 12 muffins

Caution: May require finger licking. It will come as no surprise that these muffins — although easily and inexpensively assembled with a short list of pantry staples — are a hit with anyone and everyone.

Tip: There's no need to limit the filling to jams or preserves. Consider marmalades, apple butter, jellies or nut butters for equally delicious alternatives.

- Preheat oven to 400°F (200°C)
- 12-cup muffin pan, greased

1 1/4 cups	all-purpose flour	300 mL
1 cup	whole wheat flour	250 mL
1 tbsp	baking powder	15 mL
1/2 tsp	baking soda	2 mL
1/2 tsp	salt	2 mL
2/3 cup	vegan granulated sugar or evaporated cane juice	150 mL
3/4 cup	vanilla-flavored soy yogurt	175 mL
3/4 cup	plain non-dairy milk (soy, almond, rice, hemp)	175 mL
1/3 cup	vegetable oil	75 mL
1/2 tsp	almond extract	2 mL
1/2 cup	seedless berry jam or preserves	125 mL

1. In a large bowl, whisk together all-purpose flour, whole wheat flour, baking powder, baking soda and salt.

2. In a medium bowl, whisk together sugar, yogurt, milk, oil and almond extract until well blended.

3. Add the yogurt mixture to the flour mixture and stir until just blended.

4. Divide half the batter equally among prepared muffin cups. Spoon 2 tsp (10 mL) jam into the center of each cup. Top with the remaining batter.

5. Bake in preheated oven for 21 to 26 minutes or until tops are golden and firm to the touch. Let cool in pan on a wire rack for 3 minutes, then transfer to the rack to cool.

Favorite Blueberry Muffins

Makes 12 muffins

These tender-as-can-be muffins have an easy style, their sapphire, tart-sweet berries harmonizing with a vanilla-scented batter.

Tip: When shopping for cultivated blueberries, look for the fattest berries you can find; they should be grayish purple and covered with a silvery bloom. (Wild blueberries — typically unavailable fresh in supermarkets — are tiny and almost black.) Scent makes no difference; unlike many other fruits, ripe blueberries have no fragrance.

- Preheat oven to 350°F (180°C)
- 12-cup muffin pan, greased

1½ cups	all-purpose flour	375 mL
½ cup	whole wheat pastry flour	125 mL
2½ tsp	baking powder	12 mL
½ tsp	baking soda	2 mL
½ tsp	salt	2 mL
⅔ cup	vegan granulated sugar or evaporated cane juice	150 mL
½ cup	unsweetened applesauce	125 mL
½ cup	vanilla-flavored soy yogurt	125 mL
¼ cup	vegetable oil	60 mL
1 tsp	vanilla extract	5 mL
1½ cups	blueberries	375 mL
2 tbsp	turbinado sugar	30 mL

1. In a large bowl, whisk together all-purpose flour, whole wheat pastry flour, baking powder, baking soda and salt.

2. In a medium bowl, whisk together granulated sugar, applesauce, yogurt, oil and vanilla until well blended.

3. Add the applesauce mixture to the flour mixture and stir until just blended. Gently fold in blueberries.

4. Divide batter equally among prepared muffin cups. Sprinkle with turbinado sugar.

5. Bake in preheated oven for 18 to 22 minutes or until tops are golden brown and a toothpick inserted in the center comes out clean. Let cool in pan on a wire rack for 3 minutes, then transfer to the rack to cool.

Cranberry Orange Muffins

Makes 12 muffins

With their ruby cranberries and glittering sugar tops, these muffins look labor-intensive. But they're actually a breeze to prepare. Stock up the freezer with cranberries when they are in season so you can make these year-round.

> **Tip:** Clean up as you go. In most cases, your kitchen can be completely clean by the time the muffins come out of the oven.

- Preheat oven to 375°F (190°C)
- 12-cup muffin pan, greased

1 1/2 cups	all-purpose flour	375 mL
1 1/4 tsp	baking powder	6 mL
1 tsp	baking soda	5 mL
1/2 tsp	salt	2 mL
1/2 cup	vegan granulated sugar or evaporated cane juice	125 mL
2 tsp	finely grated orange zest	10 mL
3/4 cup	freshly squeezed orange juice	175 mL
1/3 cup	vegetable oil	75 mL
1 tsp	vanilla extract	5 mL
1 1/4 cups	fresh or frozen cranberries, chopped	300 mL
1/2 cup	chopped walnuts, toasted	125 mL
2 tbsp	turbinado sugar	30 mL

1. In a large bowl, whisk together flour, baking powder, baking soda and salt.

2. In a medium bowl, whisk together granulated sugar, orange zest, orange juice, oil and vanilla until well blended.

3. Add the orange juice mixture to the flour mixture and stir until just blended. Gently fold in cranberries and walnuts.

4. Divide batter equally among prepared muffin cups. Sprinkle with turbinado sugar.

5. Bake in preheated oven for 21 to 26 minutes or until tops are golden brown and a toothpick inserted in the center comes out clean. Let cool in pan on a wire rack for 3 minutes, then transfer to the rack to cool.

Lemon Poppy Seed Muffins

Makes 12 muffins

With polka dots aplenty, these muffins will make you want to rise and shine on the grayest of mornings. A double dose of lemon (juice and zest) in the batter really makes these sing.

Tip: Substitutions are a particular temptation, and challenge, with vegan baking, as vegan cooks have become accustomed to swapping ingredients. When it comes to baking, though, stick to the recipe as much as possible, as changing too much (especially fats, sugars and leavening) can wreck the underlying chemistry of the baked goods, wreaking havoc on the end results. The best practice is to follow the recipe, period.

- Preheat oven to 400°F (200°C)
- 12-cup muffin pan, greased

2 cups	all-purpose flour	500 mL
3 tbsp	poppy seeds	45 mL
2 tsp	baking powder	10 mL
½ tsp	baking soda	2 mL
½ tsp	salt	2 mL
½ cup	vegan granulated sugar or evaporated cane juice	125 mL
⅔ cup	plain non-dairy milk (soy, almond, rice, hemp)	150 mL
⅔ cup	plain soy yogurt	150 mL
⅓ cup	vegetable oil	75 mL
2 tbsp	finely grated lemon zest	30 mL
2 tbsp	freshly squeezed lemon juice	30 mL
1 tsp	vanilla extract	5 mL

1. In a large bowl, whisk together flour, poppy seeds, baking powder, baking soda and salt.

2. In a medium bowl, whisk together sugar, milk, yogurt, oil, lemon zest, lemon juice and vanilla until blended.

3. Add the yogurt mixture to the flour mixture and stir until just blended.

4. Divide batter equally among prepared muffin cups.

5. Bake in preheated oven for 18 to 22 minutes or until tops are golden brown and a toothpick inserted in the center comes out clean. Let cool in pan on a wire rack for 3 minutes, then transfer to the rack to cool.

Banana Walnut Muffins

Makes 12 muffins

Banana two ways —
mashed and diced —
in a batter spiked with
a little nutmeg makes
these fast and easy
muffins something
special.

Tip: When you need
mashed bananas, you
can save a bowl by
mashing the bananas
in their peels. Gently
hit the unpeeled
banana against the
counter a couple of
times, then roll it back
and forth on a cutting
board, pressing down
until the peel splits.
Open the peel where it
split and scoop out the
mashed banana into a
measuring cup.

- Preheat oven to 325°F (160°C)
- 12-cup muffin pan, lined with paper liners

1 1/2 cups	all-purpose flour	375 mL
1 tsp	baking powder	5 mL
3/4 tsp	baking soda	3 mL
1/2 tsp	salt	2 mL
1/4 tsp	ground nutmeg	1 mL
3/4 cup	packed vegan light brown sugar or Sucanat	175 mL
1/2 cup	vanilla-flavored soy yogurt	125 mL
1/3 cup	vegetable oil	75 mL
1 tsp	cider vinegar	5 mL
1 cup	mashed ripe bananas	250 mL
1	large ripe banana, peeled and cut into 1/4-inch (0.5 cm) dice	1

1. In a large bowl, whisk together flour, baking powder, baking soda, salt and nutmeg.

2. In a medium bowl, whisk together brown sugar, yogurt, oil and vinegar until well blended. Stir in mashed bananas.

3. Add the yogurt mixture to the flour mixture and stir until just blended. Gently fold in diced banana.

4. Divide batter among prepared muffin cups.

5. Bake in preheated oven for 22 to 25 minutes or until tops are golden and a toothpick inserted in the center comes out clean. Let cool in pan on a wire rack for 3 minutes, then transfer to the rack to cool.

Pumpkin Spice Muffins

Makes 12 muffins

Embrace the flavors of autumn with these moist, delicious muffins. Pumpkin not only lends richness and color, but is also one of the healthiest ingredients you can keep on your pantry shelf.

Tip: An equal amount of thawed frozen butternut squash purée (sometimes labeled winter squash purée) may be used in place of the pumpkin.

- Preheat oven to 400°F (200°C)
- 12-cup muffin pan, greased

1 1/4 cups	all-purpose flour	300 mL
1/2 cup	whole wheat flour	125 mL
1 tbsp	baking powder	15 mL
2 1/2 tsp	pumpkin pie spice	12 mL
3/4 tsp	salt	3 mL
3/4 cup	vegan granulated sugar or evaporated cane juice	175 mL
1/2 cup	packed vegan dark brown sugar or Sucanat	125 mL
1 cup	pumpkin purée (not pie filling)	250 mL
1/2 cup	vegetable oil	125 mL
1/3 cup	plain non-dairy milk (soy, almond, rice, hemp)	75 mL
1/4 cup	dark (cooking) molasses	60 mL
1 tsp	vanilla extract	5 mL

1. In a large bowl, whisk together all-purpose flour, whole wheat flour, baking powder, pumpkin pie spice and salt.

2. In a medium bowl, whisk together granulated sugar, brown sugar, pumpkin, oil, milk, molasses and vanilla until well blended.

3. Add the pumpkin mixture to the flour mixture and stir until just blended.

4. Divide batter equally among prepared muffin cups.

5. Bake in preheated oven for 18 to 22 minutes or until a toothpick inserted in the center comes out clean. Let cool in pan on a wire rack for 3 minutes, then transfer to the rack to cool.

Zucchini Muffins

Makes 12 muffins

You know those gigantic zucchini your gardening friends "gift" to you at the end of the summer? Forget about using them as doorstops; shred them and make a bevy of these muffins (you can even re-gift some of them to the same friends).

> **Tip:** Any summer squash, such as yellow or pattypan, may be used in place of the zucchini. Shredded mild, sweet parsnips are also delicious.

- Preheat oven to 400°F (200°C)
- 12-cup muffin pan, greased

1 cup	all-purpose flour	250 mL
1/2 cup	whole wheat flour	125 mL
2 1/4 tsp	baking powder	11 mL
1 tsp	ground cinnamon	5 mL
1/2 tsp	baking soda	2 mL
1/2 tsp	salt	2 mL
1/4 tsp	ground nutmeg	1 mL
1/3 cup	vegan granulated sugar or evaporated cane juice	75 mL
1 cup	plain non-dairy milk (soy, almond, rice, hemp)	250 mL
1/3 cup	vegetable oil	75 mL
1 tsp	vanilla extract	5 mL
2 cups	shredded zucchini	500 mL
1 cup	chopped pecans, toasted	250 mL

1. In a large bowl, whisk together all-purpose flour, whole wheat flour, baking powder, cinnamon, baking soda, salt and nutmeg.

2. In a medium bowl, whisk together sugar, milk, oil and vanilla until well blended.

3. Add the milk mixture to the flour mixture and stir until just blended. Gently fold in zucchini and pecans.

4. Divide batter equally among prepared muffin cups.

5. Bake in preheated oven for 18 to 22 minutes or until tops are golden brown and a toothpick inserted in the center comes out clean. Let cool in pan on a wire rack for 3 minutes, then transfer to the rack to cool.

Best Bran Muffins

Makes 12 muffins

These bran muffins will impress everyone with how incredibly soft and moist they are. The secret ingredient? Soft silken tofu.

Tip: Chemical reactions start to take place as soon as you add baking powder and baking soda to the batter. Preheat the oven before you start the recipe so you can get it into the oven as soon as possible.

- Preheat oven to 400°F (200°C)
- Food processor
- 12-cup muffin pan, greased

2¼ cups	bran cereal, such as All-Bran	550 mL
⅔ cup	packed vegan light brown sugar or Sucanat	150 mL
1⅔ cups	plain soy milk	400 mL
½ cup	soft silken tofu	125 mL
⅓ cup	vegetable oil	75 mL
¼ cup	dark (cooking) molasses	60 mL
2 tsp	vanilla extract	10 mL
1 tsp	cider vinegar	5 mL
1¼ cups	all-purpose flour	300 mL
½ cup	whole wheat flour	125 mL
2 tsp	baking soda	10 mL
1½ tsp	ground cinnamon	7 mL
½ tsp	salt	2 mL
1 cup	raisins	250 mL

1. In food processor, process half the bran cereal until finely ground. Transfer to a medium bowl and stir in the remaining cereal.

2. In food processor, process brown sugar, milk, tofu, oil, molasses, vanilla and vinegar until blended and smooth. Stir into cereal. Let stand for 5 minutes.

3. In a large bowl, whisk together all-purpose flour, whole wheat flour, baking soda, cinnamon and salt.

4. Add the cereal mixture to the flour mixture and stir until just blended. Gently fold in raisins.

5. Divide batter equally among prepared muffin cups.

6. Bake in preheated oven for 16 to 21 minutes or until a toothpick inserted in the center comes out clean. Let cool in pan on a wire rack for 5 minutes, then transfer to the rack to cool.

Oat Bran Muffins

Makes 12 muffins

There's no better partner for oat bran than applesauce. Here, they team up in a simple, but always satisfying, morning muffin. For added appeal, dried cranberries are stirred into the batter.

Tip: To remove muffins from the pan with ease — especially when you're not using paper liners — keep a plastic knife on hand. Plastic knives are thin and flexible, and they don't scratch the finish on nonstick bakeware.

- Preheat oven to 350°F (180°C)
- 12-cup muffin pan, greased

1½ cups	whole wheat pastry flour	375 mL
¾ cup	oat bran	175 mL
2 tsp	baking powder	10 mL
1 tsp	ground cinnamon	5 mL
½ tsp	ground cardamom	2 mL
½ tsp	baking soda	2 mL
½ tsp	salt	2 mL
¼ tsp	ground nutmeg	1 mL
½ cup	packed vegan light brown sugar or Sucanat	125 mL
1 cup	unsweetened applesauce	250 mL
¾ cup	vanilla-flavored soy yogurt	175 mL
¼ cup	vegetable oil	60 mL
½ cup	dried cranberries	125 mL

1. In a large bowl, whisk together flour, bran, baking powder, cinnamon, cardamom, baking soda, salt and nutmeg.

2. In a medium bowl, whisk together brown sugar, applesauce, yogurt and oil until well blended.

3. Add the applesauce mixture to the flour mixture and stir until just blended. Gently fold in cranberries.

4. Divide batter equally among prepared muffin cups.

5. Bake in preheated oven for 25 to 30 minutes or until tops are golden brown and a toothpick inserted in the center comes out clean. Let cool in pan on a wire rack for 5 minutes, then transfer to the rack to cool.

Whole Wheat Morning Glory Muffins

Makes 12 muffins

Classic morning glory muffins become that much more glorious when made with whole wheat flour, plenty of fruits, vegetables and nuts, and no animal products.

Tip: Where you place muffins — or any other baked goods — in the oven makes a big difference to the end result, because different areas of the oven are different temperatures. The center of the middle rack usually has the most even temperatures. Be sure to leave at least a few inches between the oven wall and your baked item so natural hot air convection currents can bake your item evenly.

- Preheat oven to 350°F (180°C)
- 12-cup muffin pan, greased

2 cups	whole wheat pastry flour	500 mL
2½ tsp	pumpkin pie spice	12 mL
2 tsp	baking powder	10 mL
½ tsp	baking soda	2 mL
¼ tsp	salt	1 mL
⅔ cup	packed vegan light brown sugar or Sucanat	150 mL
½ cup	vegetable oil	125 mL
½ cup	carrot juice	125 mL
1 tsp	vanilla extract	5 mL
1	can (8 oz/227 mL) crushed pineapple, well drained	1
1 cup	finely shredded carrots	250 mL
½ cup	raisins	125 mL
½ cup	chopped walnuts or pecans, toasted	125 mL

1. In a large bowl, whisk together flour, pumpkin pie spice, baking powder, baking soda and salt.

2. In a medium bowl, whisk together brown sugar, oil, carrot juice and vanilla until well blended.

3. Add the oil mixture to the flour mixture and stir until just blended. Gently fold in pineapple, carrots, raisins and walnuts.

4. Divide batter equally among prepared muffin cups.

5. Bake in preheated oven for 22 to 25 minutes or until tops are golden brown and a toothpick inserted in the center comes out clean. Let cool in pan on a wire rack for 5 minutes, then transfer to the rack to cool.

Tried and True Corn Muffins

Makes 12 muffins

As moist as cake beneath their golden crust, these crumbly treats are amazing when taken in either a sweet (think jam, molasses, peanut butter) or a savory (think soup, salad, tofu scrambles) direction, but they are also wonderful on their own.

Tip: These muffins are very versatile. Try adding fresh or thawed frozen corn kernels, chopped fresh herbs (such as thyme, cilantro or basil), chopped green onions or shredded vegan cheese alternative to the batter.

- Preheat oven to 400°F (200°C)
- 12-cup muffin pan, greased

2 cups	all-purpose flour	500 mL
1 cup	yellow cornmeal	250 mL
1½ tsp	baking powder	7 mL
1 tsp	baking soda	5 mL
½ tsp	salt	2 mL
3 tbsp	vegan granulated sugar or evaporated cane juice	45 mL
1 cup	plain soy yogurt	250 mL
¾ cup	plain non-dairy milk (soy, almond, rice, hemp)	175 mL
½ cup	vegetable oil	125 mL

1. In a large bowl, whisk together flour, cornmeal, baking powder, baking soda and salt.

2. In a medium bowl, whisk together sugar, yogurt, milk and oil until well blended.

3. Add the yogurt mixture to the flour mixture and stir until just blended.

4. Divide batter equally among prepared muffin cups.

5. Bake in preheated oven for 17 to 20 minutes or until tops are light golden brown and a toothpick inserted in the center comes out clean. Let cool in pan on a wire rack for 3 minutes, then transfer to the rack. Serve warm or let cool.

Quinoa Multigrain Muffins

Makes 18 muffins

Indigenous to the Andes, quinoa was called "the mother grain" by the Incas, who considered the plant sacred. And while much has been made of quinoa's nutritional properties, its nutty flavor in this recipe is a revelation.

> **Tip:** Either white or red quinoa may be used in this recipe.

- Blender
- Two 12-cup muffin pans, 18 cups greased

½ cup	quinoa, rinsed	125 mL
⅔ cup	boiling water	150 mL
2 cups	whole wheat pastry flour	500 mL
½ cup	old-fashioned rolled oats	125 mL
2 tsp	baking powder	10 mL
1 tsp	baking soda	5 mL
1 tsp	ground cinnamon	5 mL
½ tsp	salt	2 mL
½ cup	unsweetened apple juice	125 mL
2 tbsp	ground flax seeds	30 mL
½ cup	packed vegan light brown sugar or Sucanat	125 mL
1 cup	unsweetened applesauce	250 mL
¼ cup	agave nectar	60 mL
¼ cup	vegetable oil	60 mL
½ cup	dried blueberries	125 mL

1. In a small bowl, combine quinoa and boiling water. Let stand for 20 minutes.

2. Preheat oven to 375°F (190°C).

3. In a large bowl, whisk together flour, oats, baking powder, baking soda, cinnamon and salt until blended.

4. In blender, process apple juice and flax seeds for 1 minute or until thickened and frothy. Add brown sugar, applesauce, agave nectar and oil; process for 30 seconds or until combined.

5. Add the apple juice mixture to the flour mixture and stir until just blended. Gently fold in quinoa and blueberries.

6. Divide batter equally among prepared muffin cups.

7. Bake for 18 to 23 minutes or until tops are golden and a toothpick inserted in the center comes out clean. Let cool in pans on a wire rack for 5 minutes, then transfer to the rack to cool.

Fresh Herb Muffins

Makes 12 muffins

Anyone who believes muffins are mere breakfast fare must have one of these fresh herb muffins immediately. Perfect for dinner or tucked into lunch boxes, they are a wonderful way to make homemade savory bread with little time and effort — and no yeast.

Tip: When storing fresh cut herbs in the refrigerator, gently wash them in cool water and shake the excess water from the leaves (it's fine if they're slightly damp). Wrap the herbs in paper towels and store them in the vegetable crisper.

- Preheat oven to 375°F (190°C)
- 12-cup muffin pan, greased

2 cups	all-purpose flour	500 mL
1 tbsp	baking powder	15 mL
½ tsp	salt	2 mL
¼ tsp	freshly ground black pepper	1 mL
¼ cup	chopped mixed fresh herbs (such as chives, chervil, tarragon and dill)	60 mL
1¼ cups	non-dairy milk (soy, almond, rice, hemp)	300 mL
⅓ cup	olive oil	75 mL
1 tbsp	prepared Dijon mustard	15 mL
2 tbsp	sesame seeds (optional)	30 mL

1. In a large bowl, whisk together flour, baking powder, salt and pepper. Whisk in herbs.

2. In a medium bowl, whisk together milk, oil and mustard until well blended.

3. Add the milk mixture to the flour mixture and stir until just blended.

4. Divide batter equally among prepared muffin cups. Sprinkle with sesame seeds (if using).

5. Bake in preheated oven for 18 to 22 minutes or until tops are golden and a toothpick inserted in the center comes out clean. Let cool in pan on a wire rack for 3 minutes, then transfer to the rack to cool.

NYC Coffee Cake Muffins

Makes 12 muffins

Moist and flavorful, these gorgeous, peaked muffins taste just like full-size, labor-intensive streusel coffee cake, but with minimal effort. Good luck limiting yourself to one!

Tip: It may be worth replacing your muffin pan: if your existing pan is scarred with blackened, baked-on spots, it can cause the muffins to bake unevenly.

- Preheat oven to 350°F (180°C)
- 12-cup muffin pan, greased

Topping

1 cup	packed vegan dark brown sugar or Sucanat	250 mL
1 cup	all-purpose flour	250 mL
1½ tsp	ground cinnamon	7 mL
¼ tsp	salt	1 mL
½ cup	chilled vegan margarine, cut into small pieces	125 mL

Muffins

1¾ cups	all-purpose flour	425 mL
2 tsp	baking powder	10 mL
1 tsp	baking soda	5 mL
½ tsp	salt	2 mL
1 cup	vegan granulated sugar or evaporated cane juice	250 mL
1½ cups	plain soy yogurt	375 mL
½ cup	vegan margarine, softened	125 mL
2 tsp	vanilla extract	10 mL
2 tbsp	vegan confectioners' (icing) sugar	30 mL

1. *Topping:* In a medium bowl, combine brown sugar, flour, cinnamon and salt. Using your fingers or a pastry cutter, cut in margarine until mixture resembles coarse crumbs. Refrigerate until ready to use.

2. *Muffins:* In another medium bowl, whisk together flour, baking powder, baking soda and salt.

3. In a large bowl, using an electric mixer on medium speed, beat sugar, yogurt, margarine and vanilla until light and fluffy.

4. With the mixer on low speed, beat the flour mixture into the margarine mixture until just blended.

5. Divide half the batter equally among prepared muffin cups. Sprinkle with half the topping. Top with the remaining batter and sprinkle with the remaining streusel.

6. Bake in preheated oven for 25 to 30 minutes or until a toothpick inserted in the center comes out clean. Let cool in pan on a wire rack for 5 minutes, then transfer to the rack to cool. Dust with confectioners' sugar.

Gingerbread Muffins

Makes 16 muffins

Too many ginger muffins lean toward the soothingly plain; these are the opposite of that — they're spicy with an ample amount of ginger, as well as cinnamon, allspice and cloves.

> **Tip:** To push the ginger flavor of these muffins to the max, add $1/3$ cup (75 mL) chopped crystallized ginger in step 1.

- Preheat oven to 375°F (190°C)
- Two 12-cup muffin pans, 16 cups lined with paper liners

2 cups	all-purpose flour	500 mL
$1/2$ cup	whole wheat flour	125 mL
1 tbsp	ground ginger	15 mL
$1\frac{1}{2}$ tsp	baking soda	7 mL
$1\frac{1}{4}$ tsp	ground cinnamon	6 mL
$1/2$ tsp	ground allspice	2 mL
$1/2$ tsp	salt	2 mL
$1/4$ tsp	ground cloves	1 mL
$1/2$ cup	packed vegan dark brown sugar or Sucanat	125 mL
$1/2$ cup	vegetable oil	125 mL
2 tsp	vanilla extract	10 mL
1 cup	dark (cooking) molasses	250 mL
2 tsp	cider vinegar	10 mL
1 cup	boiling water	250 mL

1. In a large bowl, whisk together all-purpose flour, whole wheat flour, ginger, baking soda, cinnamon, allspice, salt and cloves.

2. In a medium bowl, whisk together brown sugar, oil and vanilla until well blended.

3. Add the oil mixture to the flour mixture and stir until just blended.

4. In a large glass measuring cup, combine molasses and vinegar. Stir in boiling water. Slowly pour into batter, stirring until just blended.

5. Divide batter equally among prepared muffin cups.

6. Bake in preheated oven for 22 to 27 minutes or until a toothpick inserted in the center comes out clean. Let cool in pans on a wire rack for 3 minutes, then transfer to the rack to cool.

Chocolate Chip Muffins

Makes 12 muffins

Get the kids to help with these delectable muffins. They make a delicious change of pace from chocolate chip cookies.

> **Tip:** If vegan chocolate chips are hard to come by, substitute 9 oz (270 g) vegan semisweet chocolate, chopped.

- Preheat oven to 350°F (180°C)
- 12-cup muffin pan, lined with paper liners

1 cup	all-purpose flour	250 mL
1 cup	whole wheat flour	250 mL
2 tsp	baking powder	10 mL
1/2 tsp	baking soda	2 mL
1/2 tsp	salt	2 mL
1 cup	vegan granulated sugar or evaporated cane juice	250 mL
3/4 cup	plain soy yogurt	175 mL
1/2 cup	vegan margarine, melted	125 mL
2 tsp	vanilla extract	10 mL
2/3 cup	non-dairy milk (soy, almond, rice, hemp)	150 mL
1 1/2 cups	vegan semisweet chocolate chips	375 mL

1. In a large bowl, whisk together all-purpose flour, whole wheat flour, baking powder, baking soda and salt.

2. In a medium bowl, whisk together sugar, yogurt, margarine and vanilla until well blended. Whisk in milk until blended.

3. Add the yogurt mixture to the flour mixture and stir until just blended. Gently fold in chocolate chips.

4. Divide batter equally among prepared muffin cups.

5. Bake in preheated oven for 22 to 27 minutes or until tops are golden and a toothpick inserted in the center comes out clean. Let cool in pan on a wire rack for 5 minutes, then transfer to the rack to cool.

Dark Chocolate Muffins

Makes 12 muffins

A double dose of decadent chocolate renders these muffins irresistible. They're amazing plain, but try them with a spread of peanut butter or raspberry jam, too.

> **Tip:** To chop chocolate bars in no time, lightly loosen the wrapper, then whack the bar in several places with a rolling pin. Unwrap the chocolate to check your progress. If you need smaller pieces, just rewrap the bar and continue hitting it with the rolling pin.

- Preheat oven to 350°F (180°C)
- 12-cup muffin pan, greased

1½ cups	all-purpose flour	375 mL
½ cup	unsweetened cocoa powder (not Dutch process)	125 mL
1½ tsp	baking powder	7 mL
¼ tsp	baking soda	1 mL
¼ tsp	salt	1 mL
¾ cup	vegan granulated sugar or evaporated cane juice	175 mL
1 cup + 2 tbsp	plain non-dairy milk (soy, almond, rice, hemp)	280 mL
¼ cup	vegetable oil	60 mL
1 tbsp	cider vinegar	15 mL
1 tsp	vanilla extract	5 mL
3 oz	vegan bittersweet chocolate, chopped	90 g

1. In a large bowl, whisk together flour, cocoa powder, baking powder, baking soda and salt.

2. In a medium bowl, whisk together sugar, milk, oil, vinegar and vanilla until well blended.

3. Add the milk mixture to the flour mixture and stir until just blended. Gently fold in chocolate.

4. Divide batter equally among prepared muffin cups.

5. Bake in preheated oven for 18 to 22 minutes or until a toothpick inserted in the center comes out clean. Let cool in pan on a wire rack for 3 minutes, then transfer to the rack to cool.

Breakfast Muffins

Apple Berry Muffins

Makes 12 muffins

These hearty muffins are packed with good-for-you stuff: both fresh and dried fruit, whole wheat flour, old-fashioned oats, tofu and flax seeds.

Tip: These muffins are infinitely variable. Use any type of berries or chopped fruit in place of the blueberries, use any dried fruit that suits your fancy in place of the dried cranberries and swap out the almonds for any nuts or seeds you prefer.

- Preheat oven to 375°F (190°C)
- Blender
- 12-cup muffin pan, greased

Topping

2 tbsp	packed vegan light brown sugar or Sucanat	30 mL
1/4 tsp	ground cinnamon	1 mL

Muffins

1 1/4 cups	large-flake (old-fashioned) rolled oats	300 mL
3/4 cup	all-purpose flour	175 mL
1/2 cup	whole wheat flour	125 mL
2 tsp	baking powder	10 mL
1 tsp	ground cinnamon	5 mL
1/2 tsp	baking soda	2 mL
1/2 tsp	salt	2 mL
2/3 cup	vegan granulated sugar or evaporated cane juice	150 mL
3/4 cup	vanilla-flavored non-dairy milk (soy, almond, rice, hemp)	175 mL
1/2 cup	soft silken tofu	125 mL
1/4 cup	vegetable oil	60 mL
2 tbsp	ground flax seeds	30 mL
1 cup	finely chopped apple	250 mL
1 cup	blueberries	250 mL
1/3 cup	dried cranberries	75 mL
1/2 cup	sliced almonds	125 mL

1. *Topping:* In a small bowl, combine brown sugar and cinnamon. Set aside.

2. *Muffins:* In a large bowl, whisk together oats, all-purpose flour, whole wheat flour, baking powder, cinnamon, baking soda and salt.

3. In blender, process sugar, milk, tofu, oil and flax seeds for 1 minute or until thickened and frothy.

4. Add the milk mixture to the flour mixture and stir until just blended. Gently fold in apple, blueberries and cranberries.

5. Divide batter equally among prepared muffin cups. Sprinkle with topping and almonds.

6. Bake in preheated oven for 21 to 24 minutes or until a toothpick inserted in the center comes out clean. Let cool in pan on a wire rack for 3 minutes, then transfer to the rack to cool.

Whole Wheat Blackberry Crumb Muffins

Makes 12 muffins

The charm of these muffins is obvious: sweet summer blackberries are cloaked in a simple batter and baked in a hot oven so that everything good about them becomes even better.

> **Tip:** Cleaning a blender can be a chore. But there is a simple way to make the blender clean itself. Fill the pitcher halfway with hot water and add a drop of dish cleaning liquid. Cover and blend for a few seconds. Rinse out the pitcher with more hot water and dry.

- Preheat oven to 400°F (200°C)
- Blender
- 12-cup muffin pan, greased

Topping

¼ cup	packed vegan light brown sugar or Sucanat	60 mL
2 tbsp	whole wheat pastry flour	30 mL
½ tsp	ground cinnamon	2 mL
2 tbsp	vegan margarine, melted	30 mL

Muffins

1½ cups	whole wheat pastry flour	375 mL
2 tsp	baking powder	10 mL
½ tsp	salt	2 mL
3 tbsp	ground flax seeds	45 mL
⅔ cup	plain non-dairy milk (soy, almond, rice, hemp)	150 mL
⅔ cup	vegan granulated sugar or evaporated cane juice	150 mL
⅓ cup	vegetable oil	75 mL
1 cup	blackberries	250 mL

1. *Topping:* In a small bowl, combine brown sugar, flour, cinnamon and margarine until crumbly. Refrigerate until ready to use.

2. *Muffins:* In a large bowl, whisk together flour, baking powder and salt.

3. In blender, process flax seeds and milk for 1 minute or until thickened and frothy. Add sugar and oil; process for 2 minutes or until well blended and frothy.

4. Add the flax seed mixture to the flour mixture and stir until just blended. Gently fold in blackberries.

5. Divide batter equally among prepared muffin cups. Sprinkle with topping.

6. Bake in preheated oven for 18 to 22 minutes or until tops are golden brown and a toothpick inserted in the center comes out clean. Let cool in pan on a wire rack for 5 minutes, then transfer to the rack to cool.

Blueberry Lemon Muffins

Makes 12 muffins

Here, golden vanilla muffins meet sunny lemon and juicy ripe berries, to great breakfast acclaim.

Tip: To get the maximum juice from your citrus fruits before juicing them by hand, first roll them back and forth on the counter while applying slight pressure with your hand. This will loosen up the fruit and allow the juices to flow out more easily.

- Preheat oven to 400°F (200°C)
- 12-cup muffin pan, greased

1 1/3 cups	plain non-dairy milk (soy, almond, rice, hemp)	325 mL
1 tbsp	finely grated lemon zest	15 mL
2 tbsp	freshly squeezed lemon juice	30 mL
2 cups	all-purpose flour	500 mL
2 tsp	baking powder	10 mL
1/2 tsp	baking soda	2 mL
1/2 tsp	salt	2 mL
2/3 cup	vegan granulated sugar or evaporated cane juice	150 mL
1/3 cup	vegan margarine, melted	75 mL
1 tsp	vanilla extract	5 mL
1 1/2 cups	blueberries	375 mL
2 tbsp	vegan granulated sugar or evaporated cane juice	30 mL

1. In a medium bowl, combine milk, lemon zest and lemon juice. Let stand for 5 minutes or until curdled.

2. In a large bowl, whisk together flour, baking powder, baking soda and salt.

3. Whisk 2/3 cup (150 mL) sugar, margarine and vanilla into milk mixture until well blended.

4. Add the milk mixture to the flour mixture and stir until just blended. Gently fold in blueberries.

5. Divide batter equally among prepared muffin cups. Sprinkle with 2 tbsp (30 mL) sugar.

6. Bake in preheated oven for 19 to 23 minutes or until tops are golden brown and a toothpick inserted in the center comes out clean. Let cool in pan on a wire rack for 5 minutes, then transfer to the rack to cool.

Granola Dried Blueberry Muffins

Makes 12 muffins

Serve these granola muffins with more vanilla soy yogurt in a cup for a perfectly delicious, healthy breakfast.

> **Tip:** For even more rustic and extra-healthy muffins, omit the all-purpose flour and use 2 cups (500 mL) whole wheat flour.

- Preheat oven to 350°F (180°C)
- 12-cup muffin pan, greased

1 cup	whole wheat flour	250 mL
1 cup	all-purpose flour	250 mL
1 tbsp	baking powder	15 mL
1 tsp	ground cinnamon	5 mL
1/2 tsp	salt	2 mL
1 1/2 cups	vegan granola, divided	375 mL
2/3 cup	packed vegan light brown sugar or Sucanat	150 mL
3/4 cup	vanilla-flavored soy yogurt	175 mL
1/3 cup	plain non-dairy milk (soy, almond, rice, hemp)	75 mL
1/3 cup	vegetable oil	75 mL
2	large ripe bananas, diced	2
1/2 cup	dried blueberries	125 mL

1. In a large bowl, whisk together whole wheat flour, all-purpose flour, baking powder, cinnamon and salt. Stir in 3/4 cup (175 mL) of the granola.

2. In a medium bowl, whisk together brown sugar, yogurt, milk and oil until well blended.

3. Add the yogurt mixture to the flour mixture and stir until just blended. Gently fold in bananas and blueberries.

4. Divide batter equally among prepared muffin cups. Sprinkle with the remaining granola and gently press into batter.

5. Bake in preheated oven for 18 to 21 minutes or until tops are golden brown and a toothpick inserted in the center comes out clean. Let cool in pan on a wire rack for 5 minutes, then transfer to the rack to cool.

Raspberry Vanilla Muffins

Makes 12 muffins

These muffins taste like late summer. You can make them with just about any ripe berry that suits your fancy, including blueberries, blackberries or boysenberries.

Tip: When buying fresh raspberries, look for berries that are deeply colored, plump and free of hulls (hulls signal tart, unripe fruits). Avoid containers with juice stains, which may mean the berries have been crushed, and check for mold. Raspberries are very fragile; refrigerate them, unwashed (moisture speeds mold), in a single layer on a plate, covered loosely, for up to 3 days.

- Preheat oven to 400°F (200°C)
- Blender
- 12-cup muffin pan, greased

1¾ cups	all-purpose flour	425 mL
2 tsp	baking powder	10 mL
1 tsp	baking soda	5 mL
½ tsp	salt	2 mL
3 tbsp	ground flax seeds	45 mL
¾ cup	vegan granulated sugar or evaporated cane juice	175 mL
1 cup	vanilla-flavored soy yogurt	250 mL
½ cup	vegetable oil	125 mL
1 tsp	vanilla extract	5 mL
1⅓ cups	raspberries	325 mL

1. In a large bowl, whisk together flour, baking powder, baking soda and salt.

2. In blender, process flax seeds and ⅓ cup (75 mL) water for 1 minute or until thickened and frothy. Add sugar, yogurt, oil and vanilla; process for 2 minutes or until well blended and frothy.

3. Add the flax seed mixture to the flour mixture and stir until just blended. Gently fold in raspberries.

4. Divide batter equally among prepared muffin cups.

5. Bake in preheated oven for 20 to 25 minutes or until tops are golden brown and a toothpick inserted in the center comes out clean. Let cool in pan on a wire rack for 5 minutes, then transfer to the rack to cool.

Strawberry Yogurt Muffins

Makes 12 muffins

At the height of summer, you can't have too many strawberries. Here, they are enveloped in golden muffins. The slightly tangy, not-too-sweet batter is a breeze to mix up.

Tip: Although they are somewhat harder to find, almond milk yogurt or rice milk yogurt may be used in place of the soy yogurt.

- Preheat oven to 400°F (200°C)
- Blender
- 12-cup muffin pan, greased

²⁄₃ cup	vegan granulated sugar or evaporated cane juice, divided	150 mL
1 cup	all-purpose flour	250 mL
¹⁄₂ cup	whole wheat pastry flour	125 mL
1 tsp	baking powder	5 mL
¹⁄₂ tsp	salt	2 mL
¹⁄₄ tsp	baking soda	1 mL
1¹⁄₄ cups	halved strawberries	300 mL
¹⁄₃ cup	vegetable oil	75 mL
¹⁄₃ cup	vanilla-flavored soy yogurt	75 mL
1 tsp	vanilla extract	5 mL

1. Set aside 1 tbsp (15 mL) of the sugar. In a large bowl, whisk together the remaining sugar, all-purpose flour, whole wheat pastry flour, baking powder, salt and baking soda.

2. In blender, process strawberries, oil, yogurt and vanilla until blended and smooth.

3. Add the strawberry mixture to the flour mixture and stir until just blended.

4. Divide batter equally among prepared muffin cups. Sprinkle with the reserved sugar.

5. Bake in preheated oven for 19 to 24 minutes or until a toothpick inserted in the center comes out clean. Let cool in pan on a wire rack for 5 minutes, then transfer to the rack to cool.

Dried Cherry Corn Muffins

Makes 12 muffins

The crunchy, subtly spicy corn muffin base showcases the tart-sweet intensity of dried cherries.

Tip: Use any variety of dried fruit in place of the cherries.

- Preheat oven to 375°F (190°C)
- 12-cup muffin pan, greased

1¼ cups	plain soy milk	300 mL
2 tsp	finely grated lemon zest	10 mL
1 tbsp	freshly squeezed lemon juice	15 mL
1¼ cups	whole wheat pastry flour	300 mL
¾ cup	yellow cornmeal	175 mL
¾ tsp	salt	3 mL
½ tsp	baking soda	2 mL
¼ tsp	ground allspice	1 mL
¾ cup	mashed ripe bananas	175 mL
¼ cup	vegetable oil	60 mL
¼ cup	agave nectar	60 mL
⅔ cup	dried cherries	150 mL

1. In a glass measuring cup, combine soy milk, lemon zest and lemon juice. Let stand for 5 minutes or until curdled.

2. In a large bowl, whisk together flour, cornmeal, salt, baking soda and allspice.

3. In a medium bowl, whisk together bananas, oil and agave nectar until well blended. Whisk in milk mixture until blended.

4. Add the banana mixture to the flour mixture and stir until just blended. Gently fold in cherries.

5. Divide batter equally among prepared muffin cups.

6. Bake in preheated oven for 17 to 22 minutes or until tops are golden brown and a toothpick inserted in the center comes out clean. Let cool in pan on a wire rack for 3 minutes, then transfer to the rack to cool.

Apricot Muffins

Makes 18 muffins

Orange zest and agave nectar amp up the flavor of these apricot muffins. The finishing touch? A sparkling sprinkle of turbinado sugar.

Tip: Although any dried apricots will work well in this recipe, consider seeking out the organic variety. Non-organic apricots are treated with sulfur dioxide before drying. This prevents oxidation, thus preserving the fruit's rich orange color. However, the treatment produces sulfites that may trigger asthma attacks in certain people. If you are allergic to sulfites, avoid orange dried apricots. Organic dried apricots are much less pretty (they are a brownish color), but they are sulfite-free and have a subtle caramel flavor.

- Preheat oven to 350°F (180°C)
- Two 12-cup muffin pans, 18 cups greased

2 cups	all-purpose flour	500 mL
1 cup	yellow cornmeal	250 mL
2 tsp	baking soda	10 mL
1/2 tsp	salt	2 mL
2 cups	vanilla-flavored soy yogurt	500 mL
1 cup	agave nectar	250 mL
1/2 cup	vegetable oil	125 mL
2 tsp	finely grated orange zest	10 mL
1 tsp	vanilla extract	5 mL
1 cup	chopped dried apricots	250 mL
2 tbsp	turbinado sugar	30 mL

1. In a large bowl, whisk together flour, cornmeal, baking soda and salt.

2. In a medium bowl, whisk together yogurt, agave nectar, oil, orange zest and vanilla until well blended.

3. Add the yogurt mixture to the flour mixture and stir until just blended. Gently fold in apricots.

4. Divide batter equally among prepared muffin cups. Sprinkle with turbinado sugar.

5. Bake in preheated oven for 24 to 28 minutes or until tops are golden brown and a toothpick inserted in the center comes out clean. Let cool in pans on a wire rack for 3 minutes, then transfer to the rack to cool.

Georgia Peach Muffins

Makes 12 muffins

As they bake, the chunks of golden peach meld and soften, seeming to exist expressly for these muffins.

Tip: You can toast most nuts, including walnuts, pecans, almonds and pine nuts, in the microwave. To toast about a cup (250 mL) of nuts, spread them out in a single layer in a shallow bowl or a glass pie plate. Microwave on High for 3 to 4 minutes or until they're as brown as you like them. Be sure to give them a stir every minute so that they toast evenly. You can also toast sesame seeds and coconut this way; just leave them in for less time.

- Preheat oven to 400°F (200°C)
- 12-cup muffin pan, greased

1 cup	plain non-dairy milk (soy, almond, rice, hemp)	250 mL
1 tbsp	freshly squeezed lemon juice	15 mL
1 cup	all-purpose flour	250 mL
1 cup	whole wheat pastry flour	250 mL
2 tsp	baking powder	10 mL
1 tsp	baking soda	5 mL
½ tsp	ground cinnamon	2 mL
¼ tsp	salt	1 mL
¾ cup	packed vegan light brown sugar or Sucanat, divided	175 mL
½ cup	vegetable oil	125 mL
1 tsp	vanilla extract	5 mL
1½ cups	diced peeled firm-ripe peaches	375 mL
½ cup	chopped pecans, toasted	125 mL

1. In a medium bowl, combine milk and lemon juice. Let stand for 5 minutes or until curdled.

2. In a large bowl, whisk together all-purpose flour, whole wheat pastry flour, baking powder, baking soda, cinnamon and salt.

3. Whisk ½ cup (125 mL) of the brown sugar, oil and vanilla into milk mixture until well blended.

4. Add the milk mixture to the flour mixture and stir until just blended. Gently fold in peaches.

5. Divide batter equally among prepared muffin cups. Sprinkle with the remaining brown sugar and pecans.

6. Bake in preheated oven for 18 to 22 minutes or until tops are golden brown and a toothpick inserted in the center comes out clean. Let cool in pan on a wire rack for 3 minutes, then transfer to the rack to cool.

Lemon Berry Corn Muffins

Makes 12 muffins

Cornmeal gives these muffins a coarse, toothsome texture, the perfect backdrop for lush summer berries and the zing of fresh lemon.

Tip: To remove citrus zest from a Microplane or other grater, tap a pastry brush against the outside of the grater, pushing in and out to free the grated zest from the holes.

- Preheat oven to 400°F (200°C)
- 12-cup muffin pan, greased

1 cup	all-purpose flour	250 mL
1 cup	yellow cornmeal	250 mL
1 tbsp	baking powder	15 mL
½ tsp	salt	2 mL
¼ tsp	baking soda	1 mL
½ cup	vegan granulated sugar or evaporated cane juice	125 mL
¾ cup	vanilla-flavored soy yogurt	175 mL
⅓ cup	plain non-dairy milk (soy, almond, rice, hemp)	75 mL
⅓ cup	vegetable oil	75 mL
1 tbsp	finely grated lemon zest	15 mL
1¼ cups	blueberries, raspberries or blackberries	300 mL

1. In a large bowl, whisk together flour, cornmeal, baking powder, salt and baking soda.

2. In a medium bowl, whisk together sugar, yogurt, milk, oil and lemon zest until well blended.

3. Add the yogurt mixture to the flour mixture and stir until just blended. Gently fold in berries.

4. Divide batter equally among prepared muffin cups.

5. Bake in preheated oven for 20 to 25 minutes or until tops are golden brown and a toothpick inserted in the center comes out clean. Let cool in pan on a wire rack for 5 minutes, then transfer to the rack to cool.

Cardamom Orange Muffins

Makes 12 muffins

These muffins not only keep well, but their flavor intensifies over the first day or so.

> **Tip:** If you prefer, you can replace the cardamom with 1 tsp (5 mL) ground coriander or ¾ tsp (3 mL) ground nutmeg.

- Preheat oven to 350°F (180°C)
- Blender
- 12-cup muffin pan, greased

1	can (15 oz/425 mL) mandarin oranges, drained	1
2 cups	all-purpose flour	500 mL
½ cup	whole wheat flour	125 mL
1½ tsp	baking soda	7 mL
1½ tsp	ground cardamom	7 mL
½ tsp	salt	2 mL
¾ cup	vegan granulated sugar or evaporated cane juice	175 mL
½ cup	plain non-dairy milk (soy, almond, rice, hemp)	125 mL
½ cup	vegetable oil	125 mL
¼ cup	soft silken tofu	60 mL
1 tbsp	finely grated orange zest	15 mL
¾ cup	freshly squeezed orange juice	175 mL
1 tsp	vanilla extract	5 mL

1. Pat mandarin oranges dry between paper towels. Transfer to a cutting board and coarsely chop.

2. In a large bowl, whisk together all-purpose flour, whole wheat flour, baking soda, cardamom and salt.

3. In blender, process sugar, milk, oil, tofu, orange zest, orange juice and vanilla until blended and smooth.

4. Add the milk mixture to the flour mixture and stir until just blended. Gently fold in oranges.

5. Divide batter equally among prepared muffin cups.

6. Bake in preheated oven for 21 to 26 minutes or until tops are golden brown and a toothpick inserted in the center comes out clean. Let cool in pan on a wire rack for 3 minutes, then transfer to the rack to cool.

Citrus Spelt Muffins

Makes 12 muffins

Both orange zest and orange juice ensure that these muffins have ample citrus tones — a delicious complement to the nutty flavor of spelt.

Tips: When measuring flour, particularly spelt flour, be sure to spoon it into the measuring cup and level it off, rather than packing it down; this will keep these muffins light and tender.

You can keep lemons, limes and oranges for up to 1 month — ready for spur-of-the-moment muffin baking — with some special storage. Wrap each fruit individually in a sheet of newspaper. Pack them in a box or a bag and store them in a cool, dry place. Be sure to wash any ink residue off the skin before using the fruit.

- Preheat oven to 350°F (180°C)
- 12-cup muffin pan, greased

¾ cup	plain soy milk	175 mL
2 tsp	cider vinegar	10 mL
1 tbsp	finely grated orange zest	15 mL
¼ cup	freshly squeezed orange juice	60 mL
1¾ cups	spelt flour	425 mL
1 tsp	baking soda	5 mL
½ tsp	salt	2 mL
¾ cup	vegan granulated sugar or evaporated cane juice	175 mL
½ cup	vegan margarine, softened	125 mL
¼ tsp	almond extract	1 mL

1. In a glass measure, combine milk and vinegar. Let stand for 5 minutes or until curdled. Stir in orange zest and orange juice.

2. In a medium bowl, whisk together flour, baking soda and salt.

3. In a large bowl, using an electric mixer on medium-high speed, beat sugar and margarine until light and fluffy. Beat in almond extract until blended.

4. With the mixer on low speed, beat in flour mixture alternately with milk mixture, making two additions of flour and one of milk, until just blended.

5. Divide batter equally among prepared muffin cups.

6. Bake in preheated oven for 20 to 25 minutes or until tops are golden brown and a toothpick inserted in the center comes out clean. Let cool in pan on a wire rack for 5 minutes, then transfer to the rack to cool.

Tangerine Muffins

Makes 12 muffins

These fresh, sprightly muffins are so easy to make.

> **Tip:** The volatile oils in citrus zest are strongest just after zesting, so remove the zest just before adding it to the recipe.

- Preheat oven to 350°F (180°C)
- 12-cup muffin pan, greased

Muffins

1 cup	all-purpose flour	250 mL
1 cup	whole wheat pastry flour	250 mL
1½ tsp	baking soda	7 mL
½ tsp	ground cardamom	2 mL
½ tsp	salt	2 mL
½ cup	vegan granulated sugar or evaporated cane juice	125 mL
1 tbsp	finely grated tangerine zest	15 mL
1 cup	freshly squeezed tangerine juice	250 mL
½ cup	vegetable oil	125 mL
2 tbsp	cider vinegar	30 mL

Glaze

1 cup	vegan confectioners' (icing) sugar	250 mL
1 tsp	finely grated tangerine zest	5 mL
2 tbsp	freshly squeezed tangerine juice	30 mL

1. *Muffins:* In a large bowl, whisk together all-purpose flour, whole wheat pastry flour, baking soda, cardamom and salt.

2. In a medium bowl, whisk together sugar, tangerine zest, tangerine juice, oil and vinegar until well blended.

3. Add the tangerine juice mixture to the flour mixture and stir until just blended.

4. Divide batter equally among prepared muffin cups.

5. Bake in preheated oven for 24 to 28 minutes or until tops are golden brown and a toothpick inserted in the center comes out clean. Let cool in pan on a wire rack for 3 minutes, then transfer to the rack to cool while you prepare the glaze.

6. *Glaze:* In a small bowl, whisk together confectioners' sugar, tangerine zest and tangerine juice until blended and smooth. Spoon over warm muffin tops. Let cool.

Wheat Germ Banana Muffins

Makes 10 muffins

I am particularly taken with banana baked goods of all varieties, largely for their homespun flavor and lack of pretense. This version is no exception. It's a perfect muffin for starting the day — and kids love it too.

> **Tip:** You don't have to make banana muffins the moment your bananas turn brown. Instead, freeze them in a sealable plastic bag for up to 1 year. They can be thawed out in the microwave.

- Preheat oven to 400°F (200°C)
- 12-cup muffin pan, 10 cups greased

1 1/4 cups	whole wheat pastry flour	300 mL
3/4 cup	wheat germ	175 mL
2 tsp	baking powder	10 mL
2 tsp	ground cinnamon	10 mL
1/2 tsp	baking soda	2 mL
1/2 tsp	salt	2 mL
1/3 cup	vegan granulated sugar or evaporated cane juice	75 mL
1 cup	vanilla-flavored soy yogurt	250 mL
1/3 cup	vegetable oil	75 mL
1 tbsp	freshly squeezed lemon juice	15 mL
1 cup	mashed ripe bananas	250 mL

1. In a large bowl, whisk together flour, wheat germ, baking powder, cinnamon, baking soda and salt.

2. In a medium bowl, whisk together sugar, yogurt, oil and lemon juice until well blended. Stir in bananas until blended.

3. Add the yogurt mixture to the flour mixture and stir until just blended.

4. Divide batter equally among prepared muffin cups.

5. Bake in preheated oven for 20 to 25 minutes or until tops are golden brown and a toothpick inserted in the center comes out clean. Let cool in pan on a wire rack for 5 minutes, then transfer to the rack to cool.

Banana Blueberry Muffins

Makes 10 muffins

Just wonderful for any morning, any season (you can use frozen blueberries in cooler months), these homey muffins fall into the "most requested" category.

> **Tip:** Fresh blueberries freeze very well, and individually quick-frozen (IQF) berries — both wild and cultivated — are widely available. Because the berries have been frozen individually rather than as a large clump, they are perfect for baking. When blueberries are in season, you can freeze your own "IQF" berries for future muffin-making. Simply spread clean, dry berries in a single layer on a rimmed baking sheet, then freeze until solid. Transfer the berries to sealable freezer bags or airtight containers and store in the freezer for up to 6 months. When ready to use, do not thaw the berries; simply stir them into the batter gently and quickly, to avoid crushing the fruit and making the batter purple.

- Preheat oven to 375°F (190°C)
- Blender
- 12-cup muffin pan, 10 cups lined with paper liners

1½ cups	all-purpose flour	375 mL
1 tsp	baking soda	5 mL
1 tsp	baking powder	5 mL
½ tsp	salt	2 mL
¼ tsp	ground nutmeg	1 mL
2 tbsp	ground flax seeds	30 mL
¾ cup	vegan granulated sugar or evaporated cane juice	175 mL
1⅓ cups	mashed ripe bananas	325 mL
⅓ cup	vegetable oil	75 mL
1 tsp	vanilla extract	5 mL
1½ cups	fresh or frozen (not thawed) blueberries	375 mL

1. In a large bowl, whisk together flour, baking soda, baking powder, salt and nutmeg.

2. In blender, process flax seeds and 3 tbsp (45 mL) water for 1 minute or until thickened and frothy. Add sugar, bananas, oil and vanilla; process for 2 minutes or until well blended and frothy.

3. Add the flax seed mixture to the flour mixture and stir until just blended. Gently fold in blueberries.

4. Divide batter equally among prepared muffin cups.

5. Bake in preheated oven for 19 to 24 minutes or until tops are golden and a toothpick inserted in the center comes out clean. Let cool in pan on a wire rack for 5 minutes, then transfer to the rack to cool.

Pineapple Lime Muffins

Makes 12 muffins

I've always been keen on pineapple, so developing a pineapple muffin I would like was no challenge. But I think this recipe — citrusy with lime, caramely with brown sugar — is one everyone will love.

Tip: Sometimes bits of brown sugar harden into small nibs. Press the sugar through a sieve to get rid of the hard nibs so they don't create pockets in the batter.

- Preheat oven to 350°F (180°C)
- Blender
- 12-cup muffin pan, greased

1 cup	all-purpose flour	250 mL
1 cup	whole wheat pastry flour	250 mL
¾ cup	large-flake (old-fashioned) rolled oats	175 mL
2 tsp	ground ginger	10 mL
1 tsp	baking powder	5 mL
1 tsp	baking soda	5 mL
1 tsp	ground allspice	5 mL
½ tsp	salt	2 mL
2 tbsp	ground flax seeds	30 mL
1 cup	vanilla-flavored non-dairy milk (soy, almond, rice, hemp)	250 mL
2 tsp	grated lime zest	10 mL
2 tbsp	freshly squeezed lime juice	30 mL
1 cup	packed vegan light brown sugar or Sucanat	250 mL
½ cup	vegetable oil	125 mL
1	can (8 oz/227 mL) crushed pineapple, well drained	1

1. In a large bowl, whisk together all-purpose flour, whole wheat pastry flour, oats, ginger, baking powder, baking soda, allspice and salt.

2. In blender, process flax seeds, milk, lime zest and lime juice for 1 minute or until thickened and frothy. Add brown sugar and oil; process for 2 minutes or until well blended and frothy. Stir in pineapple.

4. Add the pineapple mixture to the flour mixture and stir until just blended.

5. Divide batter equally among prepared muffin cups.

6. Bake in preheated oven for 25 to 28 minutes or until tops are golden brown and a toothpick inserted in the center comes out clean. Let cool in pan on a wire rack for 5 minutes, then transfer to the rack to cool.

Persimmon Muffins

Makes 12 muffins

Fragrant persimmons star in these muffins, inspired by a classic British steamed pudding.

Tip: You'll need 3 to 4 ripe, squishy-soft persimmons for 1½ cups (375 mL) chopped.

- Preheat oven to 375°F (190°C)
- 12-cup muffin pan, greased

1 cup	plain soy milk	250 mL
1 tsp	cider vinegar	5 mL
1 cup	quick-cooking rolled oats	250 mL
1 cup	whole wheat flour	250 mL
1 tsp	baking soda	5 mL
½ tsp	ground cardamom	2 mL
½ tsp	salt	2 mL
¼ tsp	ground cloves	1 mL
⅛ tsp	ground nutmeg	0.5 mL
⅔ cup	packed vegan dark brown sugar or Sucanat	150 mL
¼ cup	vegetable oil	60 mL
1 tsp	almond extract	5 mL
1½ cups	chopped firm-ripe persimmons	375 mL

1. In a medium bowl, combine soy milk and vinegar. Let stand for 5 minutes or until curdled.

2. In a large bowl, whisk together oats, flour, baking soda, cardamom, salt, cloves and nutmeg.

3. Whisk brown sugar, oil and almond extract into milk mixture.

4. Add the milk mixture to the flour mixture and stir until just blended. Gently fold in persimmons.

5. Divide batter equally among prepared muffin cups.

6. Bake in preheated oven for 18 to 22 minutes or until tops are golden brown and a toothpick inserted in the center comes out clean. Let cool in pan on a wire rack for 5 minutes, then transfer to the rack to cool.

Fruit, Flax and Oat Muffins

Makes 12 muffins

If ever there was a reason to rise and shine, these muffins are it. They are packed with good-for-you ingredients, but what makes them stellar is their amazing taste.

Tip: Flax seeds are rich in omega-3 fatty acids, which add a health boost to muffins. However, these fats are extremely perishable and, when rancid, can actually have negative health consequences while adversely affecting the flavor of your baked goods. Store ground flax seeds in an airtight container in the freezer, where they will keep for up to 1 year.

- 12-cup muffin pan, greased

1¾ cups	plain non-dairy milk (soy, almond, rice, hemp)	425 mL
1 tbsp	cider vinegar	15 mL
1 cup	large-flake (old-fashioned) rolled oats	250 mL
½ cup	bran cereal, such as All-Bran	125 mL
¼ tsp	salt	1 mL
½ cup	boiling water	125 mL
1 cup	chopped mixed dried fruit	250 mL
⅓ cup	vegan granulated sugar or evaporated cane juice	75 mL
¼ cup	ground flax seeds	60 mL
½ cup	vegetable oil	125 mL
1½ cups	whole wheat pastry flour	375 mL
1¼ tsp	baking soda	6 mL
1 tsp	ground cinnamon	5 mL

1. In a glass measuring cup, combine milk and vinegar. Let stand for 5 minutes or until curdled.

2. In a medium bowl, combine oats, bran cereal, salt and boiling water. Stir in milk mixture, dried fruit, sugar, flax seeds and oil. Let cool.

3. Preheat oven to 375°F (190°C).

4. In a large bowl, whisk together flour, baking soda and cinnamon.

5. Add the oat mixture to the flour mixture and stir until just blended.

6. Divide batter equally among prepared muffin cups.

7. Bake for 18 to 21 minutes or until tops are golden brown and a toothpick inserted in the center comes out clean. Let cool in pan on a wire rack for 5 minutes, then transfer to the rack to cool.

Raisin Bran Muffins

Makes 12 muffins

Loaded with plump raisins and whole grains, these muffins combine the best of great taste and great nutrition.

Tip: The nutritional benefits of grapes are concentrated in raisins, making them rich in fiber, iron, selenium, potassium and B vitamins. They help to reduce cholesterol and high blood pressure and, thanks to their high natural sugar content, make an excellent post-workout snack.

- Preheat oven to 400°F (200°C)
- 12-cup muffin pan, greased

1 cup	all-purpose flour	250 mL
¾ cup	natural bran	175 mL
½ cup	whole wheat flour	125 mL
2 tsp	baking powder	10 mL
1 tsp	ground cinnamon	5 mL
½ tsp	baking soda	2 mL
½ tsp	salt	2 mL
½ cup	packed vegan dark brown sugar or Sucanat	125 mL
1¼ cups	plain non-dairy milk (soy, almond, rice, hemp)	300 mL
⅓ cup	vegetable oil	75 mL
2 tsp	cider vinegar	10 mL
1 tsp	vanilla extract	5 mL
⅔ cup	raisins	150 mL

1. In a large bowl, whisk together all-purpose flour, bran, whole wheat flour, baking powder, cinnamon, baking soda and salt.

2. In a medium bowl, whisk together brown sugar, milk, oil, vinegar and vanilla until blended.

3. Add the milk mixture to the flour mixture and stir until just blended. Gently fold in raisins.

4. Divide batter equally among prepared muffin cups.

5. Bake in preheated oven for 18 to 22 minutes or until tops are golden brown and a toothpick inserted in the center comes out clean. Let cool in pan on a wire rack for 3 minutes, then transfer to the rack to cool.

Raisin Rye Muffins

Makes 12 muffins

Raisins and rye are two great things that go great together. That being said, cranberries or dried apricots (or just about any other dried fruit) are terrific in these muffins too.

Tips: An equal amount of agave nectar or dark (cooking) molasses may be used in place of the brown rice syrup.

For a more savory muffin, use 1 cup (250 mL) chopped toasted nuts (such as pecans or walnuts) in place of the raisins.

- Preheat oven to 400°F (200°C)
- 12-cup muffin pan, greased

2 cups	rye flour	500 mL
4 tsp	baking powder	20 mL
1 tsp	ground cinnamon	5 mL
1/2 tsp	salt	2 mL
2/3 cup	plain soy milk	150 mL
1/3 cup	vegetable oil	75 mL
1/4 cup	brown rice syrup	60 mL
1 cup	raisins	250 mL

1. In a large bowl, whisk together flour, baking powder, cinnamon and salt.

2. In a medium bowl, whisk together soy milk, oil and syrup until well blended.

3. Add the milk mixture to the flour mixture and stir until just blended. Gently fold in raisins.

4. Divide batter equally among prepared muffin cups.

5. Bake in preheated oven for 15 to 20 minutes or until tops are golden and a toothpick inserted in the center comes out clean. Let cool in pan on a wire rack for 5 minutes, then transfer to the rack to cool.

Fig Date Muffins

Makes 12 muffins

Dried fruit muffins are always crowd-pleasers wherever I take them, and these dark, moist muffins are no exception. The combination of time-honored ingredients — sweet dried figs, decadent dates and crunchy walnuts — will have your friends clamoring for the recipe.

- Blender
- 12-cup muffin pan, greased

1 cup	pitted dates, chopped	250 mL
1 cup	dried figs, chopped	250 mL
1½ tsp	baking soda	7 mL
1 cup	boiling water	250 mL
¾ cup	all-purpose flour	175 mL
¾ cup	whole wheat flour	175 mL
½ tsp	baking powder	2 mL
½ tsp	salt	2 mL
3 tbsp	ground flax seeds	45 mL
½ cup	packed vegan light brown sugar or Sucanat	125 mL
¼ cup	vegetable oil	60 mL
1 cup	chopped walnuts, toasted	250 mL

1. In a medium bowl, combine dates, figs and baking soda. Stir in boiling water. Let stand for 15 minutes.

2. Preheat oven to 350°F (180°C).

3. In a large bowl, whisk together all-purpose flour, whole wheat flour, baking powder and salt.

4. In blender, process flax seeds and ⅓ cup (75 mL) water for 1 minute or until thickened and frothy. Add brown sugar and oil; process for 2 minutes or until well blended and frothy. Stir into date mixture.

5. Add the date mixture to the flour mixture and stir until just blended. Gently fold in walnuts.

6. Divide batter equally among prepared muffin cups.

7. Bake for 20 to 25 minutes or until a toothpick inserted in the center comes out clean. Let cool in pan on a wire rack for 5 minutes, then transfer to the rack to cool.

Date and Walnut Muffins

Makes 18 muffins

Here, toasted walnuts cozy up with ever-so-sweet dates for an easy and delicious muffin that manages to be both new and familiar.

Tip: Dates provide calcium, magnesium, zinc, copper, iron, selenium, potassium and polyphenols (antioxidants). Store them in an airtight container at room temperature for several months or in the refrigerator for up to 1 year.

- Blender
- Two 12-cup muffin pans, 18 cups lined with paper liners

2 cups	pitted dates, chopped	500 mL
1½ tsp	baking soda	3 mL
1 cup	boiling water	250 mL
1 cup	all-purpose flour	250 mL
½ cup	whole wheat flour	125 mL
1 tsp	ground cinnamon	5 mL
½ tsp	baking powder	2 mL
½ tsp	salt	2 mL
3 tbsp	ground flax seeds	45 mL
⅔ cup	packed vegan dark brown sugar or Sucanat	150 mL
¼ cup	vegetable oil	60 mL
1 tsp	vanilla extract	5 mL
¾ cup	chopped walnuts, toasted	175 mL

1. In a large bowl, combine dates and baking soda. Stir in boiling water. Let stand for 15 minutes.

2. Preheat oven to 375°F (190°C).

3. In a medium bowl, whisk together all-purpose flour, whole wheat flour, cinnamon, baking powder and salt.

4. In blender, process flax seeds and ½ cup (125 mL) water for 1 minute or until thickened and frothy. Add brown sugar, oil and vanilla; process for 2 minutes or until well blended and frothy. Stir into date mixture.

5. Add the flour mixture to the date mixture and stir until just blended. Gently fold in walnuts.

6. Divide batter equally among prepared muffin cups.

7. Bake for 24 to 28 minutes or until tops are golden brown and a toothpick inserted in the center comes out clean. Let cool in pans on a wire rack for 3 minutes, then transfer to the rack to cool.

Trail Mix Muffins

Makes 12 muffins

These muffins travel well and sustain travelers well, too.

Tip: Consider this recipe a template. You can use mashed banana, canned pumpkin purée (not pie filling) or mashed cooked sweet potatoes in place of the applesauce, vegan chocolate chips in place of the carob chips and the seeds, nuts and dried fruit of your liking.

- Preheat oven to 425°F (220°C)
- 12-cup muffin pan, greased

1½ cups	whole wheat flour	375 mL
½ cup	natural bran	125 mL
2 tsp	baking powder	10 mL
¼ tsp	salt	1 mL
⅔ cup	packed vegan light brown sugar or Sucanat	150 mL
1 cup	non-dairy milk (soy, almond, rice, hemp)	250 mL
½ cup	unsweetened applesauce	125 mL
¼ cup	vegetable oil	60 mL
¾ cup	carob chips	175 mL
¾ cup	lightly salted roasted sunflower seeds	175 mL
½ cup	chopped dried fruit	125 mL
1 cup	vegan granola	250 mL

1. In a large bowl, whisk together flour, bran, baking powder and salt.

2. In a medium bowl, whisk together brown sugar, milk, applesauce and oil until well blended.

3. Add the milk mixture to the flour mixture and stir until just blended. Gently stir in carob chips, sunflower seeds and dried fruit.

4. Divide batter equally among prepared muffin cups. Sprinkle with granola and press lightly into batter.

5. Bake in preheated oven for 20 to 25 minutes or until tops are golden and a toothpick inserted in the center comes out clean. Let cool in pan on a wire rack for 3 minutes, then transfer to the rack to cool.

Rhubarb Muffins

Makes 12 muffins

For sophisticated comfort, these tart-sweet muffins are hard to beat.

Tip: Rhubarb is one of spring's first treasures — look for it at the market between April and September — but you can also find it cut and frozen year-round in the frozen foods section of the supermarket.

- Preheat oven to 350°F (180°C)
- 12-cup muffin pan, greased

1½ cups	all-purpose flour	375 mL
1 cup	whole wheat flour	250 mL
2 tsp	baking powder	10 mL
1 tsp	baking soda	5 mL
1 tsp	ground cardamom	5 mL
½ tsp	salt	2 mL
2 tsp	finely grated orange zest	10 mL
¾ cup	freshly squeezed orange juice	175 mL
½ cup	unsweetened applesauce	125 mL
½ cup	agave nectar	125 mL
½ cup	vegetable oil	125 mL
1 tsp	vanilla extract	5 mL
2 cups	chopped rhubarb	500 mL
3 tbsp	turbinado sugar	45 mL

1. In a large bowl, whisk together all-purpose flour, whole wheat flour, baking powder, baking soda, cardamom and salt.

2. In a medium bowl, whisk together orange zest, orange juice, applesauce, agave nectar, oil and vanilla until well blended.

3. Add the orange juice mixture to the flour mixture and stir until just blended. Gently fold in rhubarb.

4. Divide batter equally among prepared muffin cups. Sprinkle with turbinado sugar.

5. Bake in preheated oven for 21 to 26 minutes or until tops are golden brown and a toothpick inserted in the center comes out clean. Let cool in pan on a wire rack for 5 minutes, then transfer to the rack to cool.

Sweet Potato Muffins with Dried Cranberries

Makes 12 muffins

I am an avowed fan of all things sweet potato, so it was nothing but pleasure fashioning them into a vegan muffin. These have just the right balance of sweet, tart and spice, thanks to the addition of dried cranberries, ginger and cinnamon.

- 12-cup muffin pan, greased

1/2 cup	dried cranberries	125 mL
	Hot water	
3/4 cup	all-purpose flour	175 mL
3/4 cup	whole wheat flour	175 mL
2 tsp	baking powder	10 mL
1 tsp	ground ginger	5 mL
1 tsp	ground cinnamon	5 mL
1/2 tsp	baking soda	2 mL
1/2 tsp	salt	2 mL
1/3 cup	packed vegan light brown sugar or Sucanat	75 mL
1 cup	plain non-dairy milk (soy, almond, rice, hemp)	250 mL
1/3 cup	vegetable oil	75 mL
1 tsp	vanilla extract	5 mL
1 1/2 cups	shredded peeled sweet potatoes	375 mL

1. In a small bowl, combine cranberries and enough hot water to cover. Let soak for 15 minutes. Drain well.

2. Preheat oven to 400°F (200°C).

3. In a large bowl, whisk together all-purpose flour, whole wheat flour, baking powder, ginger, cinnamon, baking soda and salt.

4. In a medium bowl, whisk together brown sugar, milk, oil and vanilla until well blended.

5. Add the milk mixture to the flour mixture and stir until just blended. Gently fold in cranberries and sweet potatoes.

6. Divide batter equally among prepared muffin cups.

7. Bake for 19 to 23 minutes or until tops are golden brown and a toothpick inserted in the center comes out clean. Let cool in pan on a wire rack for 5 minutes, then transfer to the rack to cool.

Spiced Winter Squash Muffins

Makes 12 muffins

You know how wonderful zucchini is in a sweet morning muffin or bread; now it's time to make room for winter squash at the breakfast table. You can cook your own, but for convenience, look for packages of frozen squash purée in the frozen vegetable section of the supermarket.

- Preheat oven to 350°F (180°C)
- 12-cup muffin pan, greased

1 1/2 cups	all-purpose flour	375 mL
2 tsp	baking powder	10 mL
3/4 tsp	ground cinnamon	3 mL
1/2 tsp	salt	2 mL
1/4 tsp	ground nutmeg	1 mL
1/4 tsp	ground allspice	1 mL
1/2 cup	packed vegan light brown sugar or Sucanat	125 mL
1	package (12 oz/375 g) frozen (thawed) winter squash purée	1
1/2 cup	unsweetened apple juice	125 mL
1/3 cup	plain non-dairy milk (soy, almond, rice, hemp)	75 mL
1/4 cup	vegetable oil	60 mL

1. In a large bowl, whisk together flour, baking powder, cinnamon, salt, nutmeg and allspice.

2. In a medium bowl, whisk together brown sugar, squash, apple juice, milk and oil until blended.

3. Add the squash mixture to the flour mixture and stir until just blended.

4. Divide batter equally among prepared muffin cups.

5. Bake in preheated oven for 19 to 24 minutes or until tops are golden brown and a toothpick inserted in the center comes out clean. Let cool in pan on a wire rack for 3 minutes, then transfer to the rack to cool.

Vanilla Pecan Muffins

Makes 9 muffins

Fragrant vanilla and crunchy toasted pecans turn tender muffins into little bites of comfort food, ideal straight up or with a smear of fruit jam.

> **Tip:** Walnuts and almonds garner heaps of praise for their superfood properties, but pecans are equally nutritious. They contain more than 19 vitamins and minerals, including vitamin A, vitamin E, folate, calcium, magnesium, phosphorus, potassium, several B vitamins and zinc. Pecans are also high in fiber, are a natural, high-quality source of protein and contain very few carbohydrates and no cholesterol.

- Preheat oven to 350°F (180°C)
- Blender
- 12-cup muffin pan, 9 cups greased

1 1/2 cups	all-purpose flour	375 mL
1 1/2 tsp	baking powder	7 mL
3/4 tsp	salt	3 mL
1/2 tsp	ground cardamom or ground cinnamon	2 mL
1/4 tsp	baking soda	1 mL
3 tbsp	ground flax seeds	45 mL
1/2 cup	packed vegan light brown sugar or Sucanat	125 mL
3/4 cup	vanilla-flavored soy yogurt	175 mL
1/3 cup	vegan margarine, melted	75 mL
1 1/2 tsp	vanilla extract	7 mL
1 cup	chopped pecans, toasted	250 mL

1. In a large bowl, whisk together flour, baking powder, salt, cardamom and baking soda.

2. In blender, process flax seeds and 1/3 cup (75 mL) water for 1 minute or until thickened and frothy. Add brown sugar, yogurt, margarine and vanilla; process until well blended.

3. Add the yogurt mixture to the flour mixture and stir until just blended. Gently fold in pecans.

4. Divide batter equally among prepared muffin cups.

5. Bake in preheated oven for 20 to 25 minutes or until tops are golden brown and a toothpick inserted in the center comes out clean. Let cool in pan on a wire rack for 3 minutes, then transfer to the rack to cool.

Whole Wheat Walnut Muffins

Makes 12 muffins

Tender, moist and studded with toasted walnuts, these muffins are a perfect way to welcome any morning — but especially a chilly one.

Tip: These muffins can be taken in a more sweet or more savory direction with the addition of spices or herbs. For example, add 1 tsp (5 mL) ground cinnamon, ginger or allspice for sweeter muffins; add 1 tsp (5 mL) crumbled dried sage, dried thyme or dried rosemary for more savory muffins.

- Preheat oven to 350°F (180°C)
- 12-cup muffin pan, greased

1½ cups	whole wheat flour	375 mL
1 cup	all-purpose flour	250 mL
1½ tsp	baking powder	7 mL
1 tsp	baking soda	5 mL
½ tsp	salt	2 mL
1 cup	plain soy yogurt	250 mL
½ cup	plain soy milk	125 mL
⅓ cup	vegetable oil	75 mL
⅓ cup	dark (cooking) molasses	75 mL
1 cup	chopped walnuts, toasted	250 mL

1. In a large bowl, whisk together whole wheat flour, all-purpose flour, baking powder, baking soda and salt.

2. In a medium bowl, whisk together yogurt, soy milk, oil and molasses until well blended.

3. Add the yogurt mixture to the flour mixture and stir until just blended. Gently fold in walnuts.

4. Divide batter equally among prepared muffin cups.

5. Bake in preheated oven for 24 to 28 minutes or until a toothpick inserted in the center comes out clean. Let cool in pan on a wire rack for 5 minutes, then transfer to the rack to cool.

Cinnamon Cracked Wheat Muffins

Makes 12 muffins

Don't be misled by the plain-looking appearance of these muffins: they really are fantastic. Bulgur has never tasted so delicious.

Tip: These muffins can be made with a wide variety of grains. Omit the bulgur and boiling water and substitute 1 cup (250 mL) cooled cooked grains, such as quinoa, brown rice, millet or spelt. Start the recipe with step 2.

- 12-cup muffin pan, greased

1/2 cup	bulgur (cracked wheat)	125 mL
1 cup	boiling water	250 mL
1 1/4 cups	plain soy milk	300 mL
2 tsp	cider vinegar	10 mL
1 cup	all-purpose flour	250 mL
1/2 cup	whole wheat flour	125 mL
2 1/2 tsp	baking powder	12 mL
1 1/2 tsp	ground cinnamon, divided	7 mL
1 1/4 tsp	salt	6 mL
3/4 tsp	baking soda	3 mL
1/3 cup	packed vegan light brown sugar or Sucanat	75 mL
1/4 cup	vegetable oil	60 mL
1 tsp	vanilla extract	5 mL
3 tbsp	vegan granulated sugar or evaporated cane juice	45 mL

1. In a small bowl, combine bulgur and boiling water. Let stand for 30 minutes. Drain off any excess water.

2. Preheat oven to 425°F (220°C).

3. In a medium bowl, combine soy milk and vinegar. Let stand for 5 minutes or until curdled.

4. In a large bowl, whisk together all-purpose flour, whole wheat flour, baking powder, 1 tsp (5 mL) of the cinnamon, salt and baking soda.

5. Whisk brown sugar, oil and vanilla into milk mixture until well blended.

6. Add the milk mixture to the flour mixture and stir until just blended. Gently fold in bulgur.

7. Divide batter equally among prepared muffin cups. In a small bowl, combine the remaining cinnamon and granulated sugar. Sprinkle over batter.

8. Bake for 16 to 20 minutes or until tops are golden brown and a toothpick inserted in the center comes out clean. Let cool in pan on a wire rack for 5 minutes, then transfer to the rack to cool.

Toasted Wheat Germ Muffins

Makes 18 muffins

Wheat germ, especially the toasted variety, should be a staple in everyone's refrigerator. It adds a great toasty flavor to a wealth of baked goods, can be used in place of bread crumbs in both sweet and savory dishes and is delicious sprinkled atop soy yogurt and fruit. If the flavor alone isn't convincing enough, consider the nutrition wheat germ offers (hold on to your hat): B vitamins (such as folate, niacin, thiamin and vitamin B_6), calcium, complex carbohydrates, fiber, iron, magnesium, manganese, omega-3 fatty acids, phosphorous, potassium, protein, selenium, vitamin E and zinc.

Tip: You can either use pre-toasted wheat germ in this recipe or toast raw wheat germ yourself. To toast, spread wheat germ on a large rimmed baking sheet and bake in a 350°F (180°C) oven for 5 to 8 minutes, stirring once, until golden and fragrant. Let cool completely before using.

- Preheat oven to 350°F (180°C)
- Two 12-cup muffin pans, 18 cups lined with paper liners

2 cups	whole wheat flour	500 mL
2 cups	toasted wheat germ (see tip, at left)	500 mL
2 tsp	baking powder	10 mL
1 tsp	salt	5 mL
½ tsp	baking soda	2 mL
¾ cup	vanilla-flavored soy yogurt	175 mL
⅔ cup	packed vegan light brown sugar or Sucanat	150 mL
⅓ cup	vegetable oil	75 mL
1½ tsp	vanilla extract	7 mL
1¾ cups	non-dairy milk (soy, almond, rice, hemp)	425 mL

1. In a large bowl, whisk together flour, wheat germ, baking powder, salt and baking soda.

2. In another large bowl, whisk together yogurt, brown sugar, oil and vanilla until well blended. Whisk in milk until blended.

3. Add the yogurt mixture to the flour mixture and stir until just blended.

4. Divide batter equally among prepared muffin cups.

5. Bake in preheated oven for 18 to 22 minutes or until tops are golden and a toothpick inserted in the center comes out clean. Let cool in pans on a wire rack for 3 minutes, then transfer to the rack to cool.

Morning Oatmeal Muffins

Makes 12 muffins

These muffins were an unexpected favorite at a recent brunch potluck, with guests descending in droves while they were still warm in the basket.

> **Tip:** Even if you love steel-cut oats, save them for your bowl of porridge rather than baking them into muffins; their thicker cut maintains its structure during baking, rendering tough, slightly chewy muffins.

- Preheat oven to 400°F (200°C)
- 12-cup muffin pan, lined with paper liners

1½ cups	all-purpose flour	375 mL
¾ cup	large-flake (old-fashioned) rolled oats	175 mL
1 tbsp	baking powder	15 mL
1 tsp	salt	5 mL
¾ tsp	ground cinnamon	3 mL
½ cup	packed vegan dark brown sugar or Sucanat	125 mL
1 cup	vanilla soy yogurt	250 mL
⅔ cup	vanilla-flavored non-dairy milk (soy, almond, rice, hemp)	150 mL
⅔ cup	mashed ripe bananas	150 mL
½ cup	vegetable oil	125 mL
⅔ cup	raisins	150 mL
2 tbsp	packed vegan dark brown sugar or Sucanat	30 mL

1. In a large bowl, whisk together flour, oats, baking powder, salt and cinnamon.

2. In a medium bowl, whisk together ½ cup (125 mL) brown sugar, yogurt, milk, bananas and oil until well blended.

3. Add the yogurt mixture to the flour mixture and stir until just blended. Gently fold in raisins.

4. Divide batter equally among prepared muffin cups. Sprinkle with 2 tbsp (30 mL) brown sugar.

5. Bake in preheated oven for 25 to 30 minutes or until tops are golden and a toothpick inserted in the center comes out clean. Let cool in pan on a wire rack for 3 minutes, then transfer to the rack to cool.

Amaranth Muffins

Makes 12 muffins

Amaranth is a tiny grain that dates back thousands of years to the Aztecs in Mexico. It offers a particularly high-quality protein and is also high in fiber. What I love best about it, though, is that its toasty, nutty flavor makes it a delicious (and inexpensive) alternative to nuts in a wide range of baking recipes.

- 12-cup muffin pan, greased

1 cup	raisins	250 mL
1/2 cup	whole-grain amaranth	125 mL
1/3 cup	ground flax seeds	75 mL
1 1/2 cups	boiling water	375 mL
2 cups	whole wheat pastry flour	500 mL
2 tsp	baking powder	10 mL
1 tsp	ground cinnamon	5 mL
1/2 tsp	salt	2 mL
1/2 cup	agave nectar	125 mL
1/4 cup	vegetable oil	60 mL
1 tsp	vanilla extract	5 mL
1 cup	chopped pecans, toasted	250 mL

1. In a medium bowl, combine raisins, amaranth, flax seeds and boiling water. Let stand for 20 minutes.

2. Preheat oven to 350°F (180°C).

3. In a large bowl, whisk together flour, baking powder, cinnamon and salt.

4. Stir agave nectar, oil and vanilla into raisin mixture until well blended.

5. Add the raisin mixture to the flour mixture and stir until just blended. Gently fold in pecans.

6. Divide batter equally among prepared muffin cups.

7. Bake for 20 to 25 minutes or until tops are golden and a toothpick inserted in the center comes out clean. Let cool in pan on a wire rack for 3 minutes, then transfer to the rack to cool.

Kasha Muffins

Makes 12 muffins

Stirring cooked kasha (buckwheat groats) into these muffins adds substantial nutrition benefits, along with a toasty flavor and chewy texture. Buckwheat is a very high-quality source of protein, containing all of the essential amino acids. Further, it is composed of 75% complex carbohydrates. Finally, it is wheat- and gluten-free and is high in B vitamins, phosphorus, potassium, iron and calcium.

> **Tip:** For 1 cup (250 mL) cooked kasha, you need 1/3 cup (75 mL) uncooked.

- Preheat oven to 375°F (190°C)
- 12-cup muffin pan, greased

1 1/2 cups	whole wheat pastry flour	375 mL
1/2 cup	wheat germ	125 mL
2 tsp	baking powder	10 mL
1/2 tsp	baking soda	2 mL
1/2 tsp	salt	2 mL
1 cup	vanilla-flavored soy yogurt	250 mL
1/2 cup	dark (cooking) molasses	125 mL
3 tbsp	vegetable oil	45 mL
1 cup	cooked kasha (roasted buckwheat groats), cooled	250 mL

1. In a large bowl, whisk together flour, wheat germ, baking powder, baking soda and salt.

2. In a medium bowl, whisk together yogurt, molasses and oil until well blended.

3. Add the yogurt mixture to the flour mixture and stir until just blended. Gently fold in kasha.

4. Divide batter equally among prepared muffin cups.

5. Bake in preheated oven for 19 to 23 minutes or until tops are golden and a toothpick inserted in the center comes out clean. Let cool in pan on a wire rack for 3 minutes, then transfer to the rack to cool.

Toasted Millet Muffins

Makes 12 muffins

Millet — an ancient seed originally cultivated in the dry regions of Africa and northern China — is a marvelous addition to baked goods, adding a delicate crunch akin to nuts (for a tiny fraction of the price). Don't be tempted to skip the toasting step for the millet; it takes just a few minutes and makes the millet crisp and toasty.

- Preheat oven to 400°F (200°C)
- 12-cup muffin pan, greased

2/3 cup	millet	150 mL
2 cups	all-purpose flour	500 mL
2 tsp	baking powder	10 mL
1/2 tsp	baking soda	2 mL
1/2 tsp	salt	2 mL
2/3 cup	packed vegan dark brown sugar or Sucanat	150 mL
3/4 cup	non-dairy milk (soy, almond, rice, hemp)	175 mL
3/4 cup	vanilla-flavored soy yogurt	175 mL
1/3 cup	vegetable oil	75 mL
1 tsp	vanilla extract	5 mL

1. Spread millet on baking sheet and bake in preheated oven for 2 to 3 minutes or until toasted and fragrant. Remove from oven, leaving oven on, and let cool.

2. In a large bowl, whisk together flour, baking powder, baking soda and salt. Whisk in millet.

3. In a medium bowl, whisk together brown sugar, milk, yogurt, oil and vanilla until well blended.

4. Add the yogurt mixture to the flour mixture and stir until just blended.

5. Divide batter equally among prepared muffin cups.

6. Bake in preheated oven for 18 to 22 minutes or until tops are golden brown and a toothpick inserted in the center comes out clean. Let cool in pan on a wire rack for 3 minutes, then transfer to the rack to cool.

Quinoa Power Muffins

Makes 12 muffins

Quinoa is a fast-cooking, protein-packed whole grain (technically a seed). Lightly cooked, it adds a nutty flavor and hearty texture to these super-power muffins.

> **Tip:** Use an equal amount of any chopped dried fruit of your choice in place of the dried cherries.

- Blender
- 12-cup muffin pan, greased

1 cup	unsweetened apple juice	250 mL
1/2 cup	dried cherries	125 mL
1/4 cup	quinoa, rinsed	60 mL
1 1/2 cups	soy flour	375 mL
2 tsp	baking powder	10 mL
1 tsp	ground cinnamon	5 mL
1/2 tsp	baking soda	2 mL
1/2 tsp	salt	2 mL
1 cup	plain soy milk	250 mL
1/2 cup	soft silken tofu	125 mL
1/2 cup	mashed ripe banana	125 mL
1/4 cup	agave nectar	60 mL
3 tbsp	vegetable oil	45 mL
1 tsp	vanilla extract	5 mL

1. In a small saucepan, bring apple juice to a boil over high heat. Stir in cherries and quinoa. Remove from heat and let stand for 20 minutes.

2. Preheat oven to 350°F (180°C).

3. In a large bowl, whisk together flour, baking powder, cinnamon, baking soda and salt.

4. In blender, process milk, tofu, banana, agave nectar, oil and vanilla until blended and smooth.

5. Add the milk mixture to the flour mixture and stir until just blended. Gently fold in quinoa mixture until blended.

6. Divide batter equally among prepared muffin cups.

7. Bake for 24 to 28 minutes or until tops are golden brown and a toothpick inserted in the center comes out clean. Let cool in pan on a wire rack for 5 minutes, then transfer to the rack to cool.

Maple Quinoa Corn Muffins

Makes 12 muffins

One of my vegan friends is crazy for these not-too-sweet muffins and calls them "New World Order Muffins" because they are made with three ingredients — maple syrup, quinoa and corn — that originated in the Americas.

Tip: Once opened, maple syrup should be refrigerated, preferably in a glass container. If mold develops, remove it, strain the syrup and bring it to a boil. Let cool and keep refrigerated. Maple syrup keeps indefinitely in the freezer.

• 12-cup muffin pan, greased

1 cup	quinoa, rinsed	250 mL
1 cup	yellow cornmeal	250 mL
3 tbsp	ground flax seeds	45 mL
1¼ cups	boiling water	300 mL
1¼ cups	plain non-dairy milk (soy, almond, rice, hemp)	300 mL
2 tsp	cider vinegar	10 mL
1¼ cups	all-purpose flour	300 mL
2 tsp	baking powder	10 mL
½ tsp	baking soda	2 mL
½ tsp	salt	2 mL
⅓ cup	pure maple syrup	75 mL

1. In a large bowl, combine quinoa, cornmeal and flax seeds. Stir in boiling water. Let stand for 30 minutes.

2. Preheat oven to 375°F (190°C).

3. In a glass measuring cup, combine milk and vinegar. Let stand for 5 minutes or until curdled.

4. In another large bowl, whisk together flour, baking powder, baking soda and salt.

5. Whisk maple syrup into milk mixture until well blended. Stir into quinoa mixture until blended.

6. Add the quinoa mixture to the flour mixture and stir until just blended.

7. Divide batter equally among prepared muffin cups.

8. Bake for 23 to 26 minutes or until tops are golden and a toothpick inserted in the center comes out clean. Let cool in pan on a wire rack for 3 minutes, then transfer to the rack to cool.

Muesli Muffins

Makes 12 muffins

Serve these hearty muffins, based on the traditional Scandinavian cereal, alongside a glass of orange juice or a soy latte to start the day off with both good health and great taste. You can substitute any combination of chopped dried fruit for the dried blueberries — raisins, apricots, apples, figs, cherries or cranberries are all delicious. And try almonds, hazelnuts or pepitas in place of the walnuts and sunflower seeds.

Tip: Whole wheat flour and wheat germ contain the endosperm of the wheat berry, which is high in polyunsaturated fats. These extremely perishable fats can impart off flavors and become a health hazard when they go rancid, so store whole wheat flour and wheat germ in airtight containers in the refrigerator, where they will keep for up to 6 months.

- Preheat oven to 375°F (190°C)
- 12-cup muffin pan, lined with paper liners

Muesli

½ cup	large-flake (old-fashioned) rolled oats	125 mL
½ cup	dried blueberries or cranberries	125 mL
¼ cup	chopped walnuts	60 mL
¼ cup	unsalted roasted sunflower seeds	60 mL
¼ cup	wheat germ	60 mL
2 tbsp	ground flax seeds	30 mL

Muffins

1¼ cups	all-purpose flour or whole wheat flour	300 mL
½ cup	natural wheat bran	125 mL
1 tsp	baking soda	5 mL
½ tsp	salt	2 mL
¼ tsp	ground cinnamon	1 mL
⅓ cup	packed vegan light brown sugar or Sucanat	75 mL
1 cup	mashed ripe bananas	250 mL
1 cup	unsweetened applesauce	250 mL
⅓ cup	vegetable oil	75 mL
1 tsp	vanilla extract	5 mL

1. *Muesli:* In a medium bowl, combine oats, blueberries, walnuts, sunflower seeds, wheat germ and flax seeds; set aside.

2. *Muffins:* In a large bowl, whisk together flour, bran, baking soda, salt and cinnamon.

3. In a medium bowl, whisk together brown sugar, bananas, applesauce, oil and vanilla until blended. Stir in ¾ cup (175 mL) of the muesli.

4. Divide batter equally among prepared muffin cups. Sprinkle with the remaining muesli and press lightly into batter.

5. Bake in preheated oven for 20 to 23 minutes or until tops are golden and a toothpick inserted in the center comes out clean. Let cool in pan on a wire rack for 5 minutes, then transfer to the rack to cool.

Eight-Grain Muffins

Makes 12 muffins

Looking to incorporate more whole grains into your diet? Here's my quick, easy, portable and very delicious solution.

Tip: There are many multigrain hot cereals available, such as Bob's Red Mill, Hodgson Mill, Quaker or Red River. Just be sure not to use an instant variety.

• 12-cup muffin pan, greased

1¼ cups	non-dairy milk (soy, almond, rice, hemp)	300 mL
1 tbsp	cider vinegar	15 mL
1 cup	8-grain or other multigrain hot cereal (see tip, at left)	250 mL
1 cup	whole wheat flour	250 mL
1 tsp	salt	5 mL
1 tsp	baking powder	5 mL
1 tsp	baking soda	5 mL
½ cup	packed vegan light brown sugar or Sucanat	125 mL
½ cup	unsweetened applesauce	125 mL
¼ cup	vegetable oil	60 mL
1 tsp	vanilla extract	5 mL

1. In a large bowl, combine milk and vinegar. Stir in cereal. Let stand for 20 minutes.

2. Preheat oven to 400°F (200°C).

3. In another large bowl, whisk together flour, salt, baking powder and baking soda.

4. Whisk brown sugar, applesauce, oil and vanilla into cereal mixture until well blended. Add to the flour mixture and stir until just blended.

5. Divide batter equally among prepared muffin cups.

6. Bake for 15 to 18 minutes or until tops are golden and a toothpick inserted in the center comes out clean. Let cool in pan on a wire rack for 3 minutes, then transfer to the rack to cool.

Agave Muffins

These simple muffins allow for the delicate floral notes of agave nectar to shine through.

Tip: While agave (pronounced ah-GAH-vay) is best recognized as the plant from which tequila is made, it has also been used for thousands of years as an ingredient in food. The nectar made from the plant is known in Mexico as aguamiel, or "honey water." The taste of agave nectar is comparable, though not identical, to honey. It is typically available in two varieties: light (also called amber) and dark. Either type can be used in these muffins.

- Preheat oven to 400°F (200°C)
- 12-cup muffin pan, lined with paper liners

1½ cups	all-purpose flour	375 mL
½ cup	whole wheat flour	125 mL
2½ tsp	baking powder	12 mL
½ tsp	baking soda	2 mL
½ tsp	salt	2 mL
1 cup	plain soy yogurt	250 mL
½ cup	agave nectar	125 mL
¼ cup	vegetable oil	60 mL

1. In a large bowl, whisk together all-purpose flour, whole wheat flour, baking powder, baking soda and salt.

2. In a medium bowl, whisk together yogurt, agave nectar and oil until well blended.

3. Add the yogurt mixture to the flour mixture and stir until just blended.

4. Divide batter equally among prepared muffin cups.

5. Bake in preheated oven for 15 to 18 minutes or until tops are golden and a toothpick inserted in the center comes out clean. Let cool in pan on a wire rack for 5 minutes, then transfer to the rack to cool.

French Toast Muffins

Makes 12 muffins

Here, French toast is as timeless as ever, reinvented in muffin form. You can remove the crust from the bread, but I prefer to leave it on.

Tip: For more rustic muffins, use whole wheat bread (dairy- and egg-free) in place of the white bread and substitute 1 cup (250 mL) whole wheat flour for half of the all-purpose flour.

- Preheat oven to 375°F (190°C)
- 12-cup muffin pan, greased

Topping

3½ cups	cubed firm white bread (dairy- and egg-free)	875 mL
½ cup	non-dairy milk (soy, almond, rice, hemp)	125 mL

Muffins

2 cups	all-purpose flour	500 mL
2 tsp	baking powder	10 mL
2 tsp	ground cinnamon, divided	10 mL
½ tsp	salt	2 mL
¾ cup	packed vegan light brown sugar or Sucanat	175 mL
⅓ cup	vegan margarine, melted	125 mL
1 tsp	vanilla extract	5 mL
1⅓ cups	non-dairy milk (soy, almond, rice, hemp)	325 mL
¼ cup	pure maple syrup	60 mL
2 tbsp	vegan granulated sugar or evaporated cane juice	30 mL

1. *Topping:* In a medium bowl, combine bread and milk, tossing to coat; set aside.

2. *Muffins:* In a large bowl, whisk together flour, baking powder, 1½ tsp (2 mL) of the cinnamon and salt.

3. In another medium bowl, whisk together brown sugar, margarine and vanilla until well blended. Whisk in milk until blended.

4. Add the milk mixture to the flour mixture and stir until just blended.

5. Divide batter equally among prepared muffin cups. Spoon topping evenly over batter and press lightly into batter.

6. Bake in preheated oven for 21 to 26 minutes or until a toothpick inserted in the center comes out clean. Immediately brush warm muffins with maple syrup.

7. In a small bowl, combine granulated sugar and the remaining cinnamon. Sprinkle over muffins. Let cool in pan on a wire rack for 3 minutes, then transfer to the rack to cool slightly. Serve warm.

Coffeehouse Muffins

Apple Crumb Muffins

Makes 12 muffins

Moist and delectable, these homey muffins — reminiscent of apple streusel pie — have a lovely balance of fall flavors. An equal amount of pears can be used in place of the apples.

> **Tip:** If you have trouble removing muffins from the pan (when the cups are greased, not paper-lined), set the still-hot pan on a well-dampened dish towel for 5 minutes. The steam generated will help release the efforts of your hard work!

- Preheat oven to 400°F (200°C)
- 12-cup muffin pan, greased

Topping

1/4 cup	all-purpose flour	60 mL
1/4 cup	packed vegan light brown sugar or Sucanat	60 mL
1/2 tsp	ground cinnamon	2 mL
3 tbsp	vegetable oil	45 mL

Muffins

1 1/2 cups	all-purpose flour	375 mL
1 1/2 tsp	baking powder	7 mL
1 tsp	ground cinnamon	5 mL
3/4 tsp	baking soda	3 mL
1/2 tsp	salt	2 mL
1/2 tsp	ground allspice	2 mL
1/4 tsp	ground nutmeg	1 mL
1/3 cup	vegan granulated sugar or evaporated cane juice	75 mL
3/4 cup	vanilla-flavored soy yogurt	175 mL
3/4 cup	unsweetened apple juice	175 mL
1/3 cup	vegetable oil	75 mL
1 tsp	vanilla extract	5 mL

1. *Topping:* In a small bowl, combine flour, brown sugar and cinnamon. Drizzle with oil, tossing with a fork until crumbly. Set aside.

2. *Muffins:* In a large bowl, whisk together flour, baking powder, cinnamon, baking soda, salt, allspice and nutmeg.

3. In a medium bowl, whisk together sugar, yogurt, apple juice, oil and vanilla until well blended.

4. Add the yogurt mixture to the flour mixture and stir until just blended.

5. Divide batter equally among prepared muffin cups. Sprinkle with topping.

6. Bake in preheated oven for 18 to 22 minutes or until tops are golden brown and a toothpick inserted in the center comes out clean. Let cool in pan on a wire rack for 5 minutes, then transfer to the rack to cool.

Caramel Apple Muffins

Makes 24 muffins

Here, caramel apples are all grown up in a fabulous muffin. Dark brown sugar and spices balance the tart sweetness of apple for a harmony of flavor.

Tip: To chop nuts quickly, place them in a sealable plastic bag, seal it and use a wooden kitchen mallet to break them into pieces. Just a few strikes with the mallet, and the nuts are chopped.

- Two 12-cup muffin pans, greased

1 cup	shredded apples	250 mL
1 cup	raisins	250 mL
1 cup	packed vegan dark brown sugar or Sucanat	250 mL
1/2 cup	vegan margarine	125 mL
1 tsp	ground cinnamon	5 mL
1 tsp	ground nutmeg	5 mL
1/4 tsp	ground cloves	1 mL
1 3/4 cups	all-purpose flour	425 mL
2 tsp	pumpkin pie spice	10 mL
1 tsp	baking powder	5 mL
1/4 tsp	salt	1 mL
1/2 cup	chopped pecans, toasted	125 mL

1. In a saucepan, combine apples, raisins, brown sugar, margarine, cinnamon, nutmeg, cloves and 1/2 cup (125 mL) water. Bring to a boil over medium-high heat, stirring until sugar is dissolved. Remove from heat and let cool.

2. Preheat oven to 350°F (180°C).

3. In a large bowl, whisk together flour, pumpkin pie spice, baking powder and salt.

4. Add the apple mixture to the flour mixture and stir until just blended. Gently fold in pecans.

5. Divide batter equally among prepared muffin cups.

6. Bake for 20 to 25 minutes or until a toothpick inserted in the center comes out clean. Let cool in pans on a wire rack for 5 minutes, then transfer to the rack to cool.

Vanilla Pear Streusel Muffins

Makes 12 muffins

Looking for the perfect brunch muffin to impress some guests? These muffins have sophisticated flavors, but they are still a snap to make.

> **Tip:** To ripen pears slightly, wrap them in a brown paper bag (not plastic) and leave them in a cool, dark place for a few days. The aim is to increase the concentration of ethylene gases that pears naturally emit. A pear should ripen slowly. When it yields to the touch at the neck, you have a ripe, juicy pear.

- Preheat oven to 375°F (190°C)
- 12-cup muffin pan, greased

Streusel

2/3 cup	all-purpose flour	150 mL
1/3 cup	packed vegan dark brown sugar or Sucanat	75 mL
1/2 tsp	ground cinnamon	2 mL
1/4 cup	vegan margarine, melted	60 mL

Muffins

2 cups	all-purpose flour	500 mL
2 tsp	baking powder	10 mL
1/2 tsp	baking soda	2 mL
1/2 tsp	salt	2 mL
2/3 cup	vegan granulated sugar or evaporated cane juice	150 mL
3/4 cup	plain non-dairy milk (soy, almond, rice, hemp)	175 mL
3/4 cup	plain soy yogurt	175 mL
1/3 cup	vegetable oil	75 mL
2 tsp	vanilla extract	10 mL
1 1/2 cups	diced peeled firm-ripe pears	375 mL

1. *Streusel:* In a medium bowl, whisk together flour, brown sugar and cinnamon. Drizzle with margarine, tossing with a fork until crumbly. Refrigerate until ready to use.

2. *Muffins:* In a large bowl, whisk together flour, baking powder, baking soda and salt.

3. In a medium bowl, whisk together sugar, milk, yogurt, oil and vanilla until well blended.

4. Add the milk mixture to the flour mixture and stir until just blended. Gently fold in pears.

5. Divide batter equally among prepared muffin cups. Sprinkle with streusel.

6. Bake in preheated oven for 24 to 28 minutes or until tops are golden brown and a toothpick inserted in the center comes out clean. Let cool in pan on a wire rack for 5 minutes, then transfer to the rack to cool.

Cherry Hazelnut Muffins

Makes 12 muffins

Just a few years ago, I had to make a special trek to gourmet stores to find shelled hazelnuts. But now I can find them — shelled and chopped — in the baking aisle of all my local supermarkets. Here they share center stage with sweet-tart fresh cherries.

- Preheat oven to 400°F (200°C)
- 12-cup muffin pan, greased

2 cups	all-purpose flour	500 mL
2 tsp	baking powder	10 mL
½ tsp	baking soda	2 mL
½ tsp	salt	2 mL
⅓ cup	vegan granulated sugar or evaporated cane juice	75 mL
¾ cup	plain non-dairy milk (soy, almond, rice, hemp)	175 mL
¾ cup	vanilla-flavored soy yogurt	175 mL
⅓ cup	vegetable oil	75 mL
1 cup	chopped hazelnuts, toasted	250 mL
1 cup	chopped pitted cherries	250 mL

1. In a large bowl, whisk together flour, baking powder, baking soda and salt.

2. In a medium bowl, whisk together sugar, milk, yogurt and oil until well blended.

3. Add the milk mixture to the flour mixture and stir until just blended. Gently fold in hazelnuts and cherries.

4. Divide batter equally among prepared muffin cups.

5. Bake in preheated oven for 18 to 22 minutes or until tops are golden brown and a toothpick inserted in the center comes out clean. Let cool in pan on a wire rack for 3 minutes, then transfer to the rack to cool.

Fresh Plum Muffins with Walnut Sugar Tops

Makes 10 muffins

These muffins would be terrific made with any type of stone fruit — peaches, nectarines, apricots — so feel free to substitute your summertime favorites for the plums.

Tip: To find a ripe plum, hold one in the palm of your hand. It should feel heavy. There should be some give, particularly at the blossom end (opposite the stem end). Hard plums will soften a little in a brown paper bag at room temperature within 2 days. But plums won't sweeten appreciably after they're picked: the sugars must develop on the tree.

- Preheat oven to 350°F (180°C)
- 12-cup muffin pan, 10 cups lined with paper liners

Topping

1/2 cup	finely chopped walnuts	125 mL
2 tbsp	vegan granulated sugar or evaporated cane juice	30 mL
1/4 tsp	ground nutmeg	1 mL

Muffins

1 cup	whole wheat pastry flour	250 mL
1 cup	all-purpose flour	250 mL
2 1/2 tsp	baking powder	12 mL
1/2 tsp	ground cinnamon	2 mL
1/2 tsp	baking soda	2 mL
1/2 tsp	salt	2 mL
3/4 cup	vanilla-flavored soy yogurt	175 mL
1/2 cup	agave nectar	125 mL
1/4 cup	vegetable oil	60 mL
1 tsp	vanilla extract	5 mL
1 1/2 cups	diced firm-ripe plums	375 mL

1. *Topping:* In a small bowl, combine walnuts, sugar and nutmeg. Set aside.

2. *Muffins:* In a large bowl, whisk together whole wheat pastry flour, all-purpose flour, baking powder, cinnamon, baking soda and salt.

3. In a medium bowl, whisk together yogurt, agave nectar, oil and vanilla until well blended.

4. Add the yogurt mixture to the flour mixture and stir until just blended. Gently fold in plums.

5. Divide batter equally among prepared muffin cups. Sprinkle with topping.

6. Bake in preheated oven for 20 to 25 minutes or until tops are golden brown and a toothpick inserted in the center comes out clean. Let cool in pan on a wire rack for 3 minutes, then transfer to the rack to cool.

Lemon Polenta Muffins

Makes 12 muffins

Cornmeal — preferably stone-ground — gives these muffins a crunchy texture; a sweet-tangy glaze dresses them up for Sunday brunch. Although olive oil adds great flavor, you can certainly use vegetable oil in its place.

> **Tip:** When grating lemon zest, you want just the thin yellow top coat of the skin. Overzealous grating will result in bitter flavors.

- Preheat oven to 400°F (200°C)
- 12-cup muffin pan, greased

Muffins

1 cup	all-purpose flour	250 mL
1 cup	yellow cornmeal, preferably stone-ground	250 mL
1 tbsp	baking powder	15 mL
½ tsp	salt	2 mL
⅓ cup	vegan granulated sugar or evaporated cane juice	75 mL
½ cup	olive oil	125 mL
½ cup	plain non-dairy milk (soy, almond, rice, hemp)	125 mL
⅓ cup	plain soy yogurt	75 mL
2 tbsp	finely grated lemon zest	30 mL
1 tsp	vanilla extract	5 mL

Glaze

¾ cup	vegan confectioners' (icing) sugar	175 mL
1 tbsp	freshly squeezed lemon juice	15 mL

1. *Muffins:* In a large bowl, whisk together flour, cornmeal, baking powder and salt.

2. In a medium bowl, whisk together sugar, oil, milk, yogurt, lemon zest and vanilla until blended.

3. Add the milk mixture to the flour mixture and stir until just blended.

4. Divide batter equally among prepared muffin cups.

5. Bake in preheated oven for 20 to 25 minutes or until tops are golden brown and a toothpick inserted in the center comes out clean. Let cool in pan on a wire rack for 5 minutes, then transfer to the rack to cool while you prepare the glaze.

6. *Glaze:* In a small bowl, whisk together confectioners' sugar and lemon juice until blended and smooth. Spoon over warm muffin tops. Let cool.

Banana Split Muffins

Makes 10 muffins

Bananas, chocolate, cherries and coconut have a natural affinity for each other, so it's no surprise that they are so popular in ice cream sundae form. The same flavors are equally enchanting in decadent muffins. Be sure to use very ripe bananas to get the most banana flavor.

Tip: Brown bananas are best for baking, as they are the sweetest. If your bananas aren't ripe enough, peel and bake the fruit at 450°F (230°C) on an ungreased baking sheet for 10 to 15 minutes.

- Preheat oven to 375°F (190°C)
- Blender
- 12-cup muffin pan, 10 cups lined with paper liners

1½ cups	all-purpose flour	375 mL
1 tsp	baking soda	5 mL
1 tsp	baking powder	5 mL
½ tsp	salt	2 mL
½ cup	vegan granulated sugar or evaporated cane juice	150 mL
1⅓ cups	mashed ripe bananas	325 mL
⅓ cup	vegetable oil	75 mL
⅓ cup	non-dairy milk (soy, almond, rice, hemp)	75 mL
1 tsp	vanilla extract	5 mL
½ cup	vegan semisweet chocolate chips, coarsely chopped	125 mL
½ cup	dried cherries or cranberries	125 mL
1 cup	sweetened flaked coconut, divided	250 mL
¼ cup	chopped pecans, walnuts or peanuts (optional)	60 mL

1. In a large bowl, whisk together flour, baking soda, baking powder and salt.

2. In a medium bowl, whisk together sugar, bananas, oil, milk and vanilla until well blended.

3. Add the banana mixture to the flour mixture and stir until just blended. Gently fold in chocolate chips, cherries and half the coconut.

4. Divide batter equally among prepared muffin cups. Sprinkle with pecans and the remaining coconut and press lightly into batter.

5. Bake in preheated oven for 19 to 24 minutes or until tops are golden and a toothpick inserted in the center comes out clean. Let cool in pan on a wire rack for 5 minutes, then transfer to the rack to cool.

Banana Chocolate Chip Teff Muffins

Makes 16 muffins

Teff flour lends a springy texture to a newfangled take on a favorite flavor combination. A dash of cinnamon adds a spicy-sweet note to these delectable chocolate-flecked muffins.

> **Tip:** Look for teff flour in the health food section of well-stocked grocery stores, at natural foods stores and from online flour purveyors.

- Preheat oven to 375°F (190°C)
- Two 12-cup muffin pans, 16 cups greased

1½ cups	whole wheat pastry flour	375 mL
1⅓ cups	teff flour	325 mL
2 tsp	baking powder	10 mL
1 tsp	ground cinnamon	5 mL
1 tsp	baking soda	5 mL
1 tsp	salt	5 mL
⅔ cup	packed vegan light brown sugar or Sucanat	150 mL
2 cups	mashed ripe bananas	500 mL
1 cup	plain non-dairy milk (soy, almond, rice, hemp)	250 mL
¼ cup	vegetable oil	60 mL
1 tsp	vanilla extract	5 mL
1 cup	vegan miniature semisweet chocolate chips	250 mL

1. In a large bowl, whisk together whole wheat pastry flour, teff flour, baking powder, cinnamon, baking soda and salt.

2. In a medium bowl, whisk together brown sugar, bananas, milk, oil and vanilla until well blended.

3. Add the banana mixture to the flour mixture and stir until just blended. Gently fold in chocolate chips.

4. Divide batter equally among prepared muffin cups.

5. Bake in preheated oven for 20 to 25 minutes or until tops are golden brown and a toothpick inserted in the center comes out clean. Let cool in pans on a wire rack for 5 minutes, then transfer to the rack to cool.

Tropical Fruit Muffins with Coconut Streusel

Makes 12 muffins

These showy muffins have much to offer: an assortment of tropical fruits, a vanilla-lime batter and crisp coconut topping.

Tip: For even more tropical flavor, substitute an equal amount of unsweetened coconut milk for the plain non-dairy milk.

- Preheat oven to 375°F (190°C)
- 12-cup muffin pan, greased

Streusel

1/3 cup	firmly packed vegan light brown sugar	75 mL
1/3 cup	all-purpose flour	75 mL
1/4 cup	vegan margarine, melted	60 mL
1/2 cup	sweetened flaked or shredded coconut	125 mL

Muffins

2 cups	all-purpose flour	500 mL
2 tsp	baking powder	10 mL
1/2 tsp	baking soda	2 mL
1/2 tsp	salt	2 mL
2/3 cup	vegan granulated sugar or evaporated cane juice	150 mL
3/4 cup	plain non-dairy milk (soy, almond, rice, hemp)	175 mL
3/4 cup	plain soy yogurt	175 mL
1/3 cup	vegetable oil	75 mL
1 tbsp	freshly squeezed lime juice	15 mL
1 tsp	vanilla extract	5 mL
1 cup	dried tropical fruit bits	250 mL

1. *Streusel:* In a small bowl, combine brown sugar and flour. Drizzle with margarine, tossing with a fork until crumbly. Stir in coconut. Refrigerate until ready to use.

2. *Muffins:* In a large bowl, whisk together flour, baking powder, baking soda and salt.

3. In a medium bowl, whisk together sugar, milk, yogurt, oil, lime juice and vanilla until blended.

4. Add the milk mixture to the flour mixture and stir until just blended. Gently fold in fruit bits.

5. Divide batter equally among prepared muffin cups. Sprinkle with streusel.

6. Bake in preheated oven for 18 to 22 minutes or until tops are golden brown and a toothpick inserted in the center comes out clean. Let cool in pan on a wire rack for 5 minutes, then transfer to the rack to cool.

Mango Muffins with Cardamom Crumble

Makes 12 muffins

Indian ingredients — mango, cardamom and yogurt — make these otherwise humble muffins something special.

Tip: To choose a good mango, smell it. It should have a faintly sweet aroma, especially around the stem. No perfume generally means no flavor. If the fruit smells sour or like alcohol, it's past its prime. Choose firm fruit that is just beginning to show some yellow or red in the skin. The skin should be tight around the flesh; loose skin means the mango is old.

- Preheat oven to 350°F (180°C)
- 12-cup muffin pan, lined with paper liners

Crumble

1 cup	slivered almonds	250 mL
¼ cup	packed vegan light brown sugar or Sucanat	60 mL
½ tsp	ground cardamom	2 mL

Muffins

2 cups	all-purpose flour	500 mL
1 tsp	baking powder	5 mL
1 tsp	baking soda	5 mL
1 tsp	ground ginger	5 mL
½ tsp	ground cardamom	2 mL
½ tsp	salt	2 mL
¾ cup	vegan granulated sugar or evaporated cane juice	175 mL
1½ cups	vanilla-flavored soy yogurt	375 mL
⅓ cup	vegetable oil	75 mL
⅓ cup	unsweetened applesauce	75 mL
1½ cups	diced firm-ripe mangos	375 mL

1. *Crumble:* In a small bowl, combine almonds, brown sugar and cardamom. Set aside.

2. *Muffins:* In a large bowl, whisk together flour, baking powder, baking soda, ginger, cardamom and salt.

3. In a medium bowl, whisk together sugar, yogurt, oil and applesauce until well blended.

4. Add the yogurt mixture to the flour mixture and stir until just blended. Gently fold in mangos.

5. Divide batter equally among prepared muffin cups. Sprinkle with crumble.

6. Bake in preheated oven for 20 to 25 minutes or until tops are golden brown and a toothpick inserted in the center comes out clean. Let cool in pan on a wire rack for 5 minutes, then transfer to the rack to cool.

Lemon Poppy Seed Muffins (page 28)
and Cranberry Orange Muffins (page 27)

Dark Chocolate Muffins (page 42)

Pineapple Lime Muffins (page 60)

Strawberry Yogurt Muffins (page 50)

French Toast Muffins (page 84)

Trail Mix Muffins (page 67)

Fresh Plum Muffins with
Walnut Sugar Tops (page 90)

Tropical Fruit Muffins with Coconut Streusel (page 94)

Chocolate Chip Coffee Cake Muffins (page 110)

Jelly Doughnut Muffins (page 97)
and Chai Latte Muffins (page 107)

Sweet Potato Sage Muffins (page 142)

Ancho Chile and Cherry Tomato Muffins (page 137)

Spiced Pistachio Muffins (page 145)

Rum and Coconut Muffins (page 157)
and Citrus Olive Oil Muffins (page 162)

Gajar Halvah Muffins (page 179)

Rugalach Muffins (page 170)

Jelly Doughnut Muffins

Makes 10 muffins

These fabulous muffins require no explanation. Frankly, they are far more delicious than anything you could find at the local doughnut shop.

Tip: You can make your own muffin liners: cut a piece of foil into small squares and mold each square on the outside of a muffin cup. Insert the molded foils into the muffin cups and fill them with batter.

- Preheat oven to 350°F (180°C)
- 12-cup muffin pan, 10 cups lined with paper liners

1¾ cups	all-purpose flour	425 mL
1¼ tsp	baking powder	6 mL
½ tsp	baking soda	2 mL
½ tsp	salt	2 mL
½ tsp	ground nutmeg	2 mL
½ cup	vegan granulated sugar or evaporated cane juice	125 mL
1 cup	vanilla-flavored soy yogurt	250 mL
⅓ cup	vegetable oil	75 mL
½ cup	seedless raspberry preserves	125 mL

Topping

¼ cup	vegan granulated sugar or evaporated cane juice	60 mL
1 tsp	ground cinnamon	5 mL
¼ cup	vegan margarine, melted	60 mL

1. *Muffins:* In a large bowl, whisk together flour, baking powder, baking soda, salt and nutmeg.

2. In a medium bowl, whisk together sugar, yogurt and oil until well blended.

3. Add the yogurt mixture to the flour mixture and stir until just blended.

4. Divide batter equally among prepared muffin cups. Spoon 2 tsp (10 mL) preserves in the center of each cup (the preserves will sink as the muffins bake).

5. Bake in preheated oven for 20 to 25 minutes or until tops are golden and spring back when touched. Let cool in pan on a wire rack for 5 minutes, then transfer to the rack.

6. *Topping:* In a small bowl, combine sugar and cinnamon. Generously brush warm muffin tops with margarine, then sprinkle with cinnamon mixture. Let cool.

Chocolate Avocado Muffins

Makes 12 muffins

Avocado replaces the eggs and most of the oil in a rich, chocolaty batter that turns out super-moist muffins.

Tip: Although avocados don't freeze well whole or sliced, I've found that nicely ripe (but not overripe) ones can be frozen for up to 5 months if they're first peeled, seeded and mashed like guacamole with about 1½ tsp (7 mL) freshly squeezed lemon or lime juice per avocado. The California Avocado Board recommends this method too. Freeze the avocado mash in airtight plastic containers with very little air space.

- Preheat oven to 350°F (180°C)
- Blender
- 12-cup muffin pan, greased

¾ cup	all-purpose flour	175 mL
¾ cup	whole wheat flour	175 mL
¾ cup	unsweetened cocoa powder (not Dutch process)	175 mL
1 tsp	baking powder	5 mL
¾ tsp	baking soda	3 mL
¾ tsp	salt	3 mL
1	ripe Haas avocado, chopped	1
1 cup	brown rice syrup	250 mL
¾ cup	plain soy milk	175 mL
⅓ cup	vegetable oil	75 mL
1 tsp	vanilla extract	5 mL

1. In a large bowl, whisk together all-purpose flour, whole wheat flour, cocoa powder, baking powder, baking soda and salt.

2. In blender, process avocado, syrup, soy milk, oil and vanilla until blended and smooth.

3. Add the avocado mixture to the flour mixture and stir until just blended.

4. Divide batter equally among prepared muffin cups.

5. Bake in preheated oven for 22 to 27 minutes or until a toothpick inserted in the center comes out clean. Let cool in pan on a wire rack for 5 minutes, then transfer to the rack to cool.

Carrot Cake Muffins

Makes 12 muffins

Carrot cake is every bit as American as apple pie. Here, I use it as inspiration for a healthy muffin that is moist, heady with spices and just plain good!

Tip: It may sound unusual, but shredded parsnips make an excellent substitution for the carrots in this recipe. Equally moist, they are actually sweeter than carrots once cooked or baked.

- Preheat oven to 400°F (200°C)
- 12-cup muffin pan, greased

1 cup	all-purpose flour	250 mL
½ cup	whole wheat flour	125 mL
2 tsp	baking powder	10 mL
1 tsp	ground cinnamon	5 mL
½ tsp	baking soda	2 mL
½ tsp	salt	2 mL
½ tsp	ground ginger	2 mL
¼ tsp	ground nutmeg	1 mL
½ cup	packed vegan light brown sugar or Sucanat	125 mL
1 cup	plain non-dairy milk (soy, almond, rice, hemp)	250 mL
⅓ cup	vegan margarine, melted	75 mL
1 tsp	vanilla extract	5 mL
2 cups	shredded carrots	500 mL
½ cup	dried currants	125 mL
½ cup	chopped walnuts or pecans	125 mL

1. In a large bowl, whisk together all-purpose flour, whole wheat flour, baking powder, cinnamon, baking soda, salt, ginger and nutmeg.

2. In a medium bowl, whisk together brown sugar, milk, margarine and vanilla until well blended.

3. Add the milk mixture to the flour mixture and stir until just blended. Gently fold in carrots and currants.

4. Divide batter equally among prepared muffin cups. Sprinkle with walnuts.

5. Bake in preheated oven for 18 to 22 minutes or until tops are golden brown and a toothpick inserted in the center comes out clean. Let cool in pan on a wire rack for 3 minutes, then transfer to the rack to cool.

Toasted Almond Muffins

Makes 12 muffins

Here, toasty almonds are framed by a scrumptious brown sugar batter that underlines their refined nuttiness.

Tip: For more decadent coffeetime muffins, decrease the non-dairy milk to 1/3 cup (75 mL) and replace the vegetable oil with 1/2 cup (125 mL) vegan margarine, melted.

- Preheat oven to 400°F (200°C)
- 12-cup muffin pan, greased

1 1/2 cups	all-purpose flour	375 mL
1/2 cup	whole wheat flour	125 mL
2 tsp	baking powder	10 mL
1/2 tsp	baking soda	2 mL
1/2 tsp	salt	2 mL
1/3 cup	packed vegan light brown sugar or Sucanat	75 mL
1 cup	plain soy yogurt	250 mL
1/2 cup	plain non-dairy milk (soy, almond, rice, hemp)	125 mL
1/3 cup	vegetable oil	75 mL
1 tsp	almond extract	5 mL
1/2 cup	sliced almonds	125 mL

1. In a large bowl, whisk together all-purpose flour, whole wheat flour, baking powder, baking soda and salt.

2. In a medium bowl, whisk together brown sugar, yogurt, milk, oil and almond extract until well blended.

3. Add the yogurt mixture to the flour mixture and stir until just blended.

4. Divide batter equally among prepared muffin cups. Sprinkle with almonds.

5. Bake in preheated oven for 18 to 22 minutes or until tops are golden brown and a toothpick inserted in the center comes out clean. Let cool in pan on a wire rack for 5 minutes, then transfer to the rack to cool.

Almond Poppy Seed Muffins

Makes 12 muffins

Poppy seeds add a subtle crunch here, a foil for the brown sugar batter and almond fragrance.

> **Tip:** Poppy seeds are more than polka-dot adornment; they provide many minerals, including manganese, calcium, phosphorus, copper, iron and zinc. Because of their high oil content, they can turn rancid quickly, particularly if stored at room temperature. To keep them fresh, store them in an airtight container in the refrigerator or freezer.

- Preheat oven to 400°F (200°C)
- 12-cup muffin pan, greased

1¾ cups	all-purpose flour	425 mL
2 tbsp	poppy seeds	30 mL
1 tbsp	baking powder	15 mL
½ tsp	salt	2 mL
¼ tsp	baking soda	1 mL
⅓ cup	packed vegan light brown sugar or Sucanat	75 mL
¾ cup	plain non-dairy milk (soy, almond, rice, hemp)	175 mL
¾ cup	vanilla-flavored soy yogurt	175 mL
⅓ cup	vegetable oil	75 mL
1 tsp	almond extract	5 mL

1. In a large bowl, whisk together flour, poppy seeds, baking powder, salt and baking soda.

2. In a medium bowl, whisk together brown sugar, milk, yogurt, oil and almond extract until well blended.

3. Add the yogurt mixture to the flour mixture and stir until just blended.

4. Divide batter equally among prepared muffin cups.

5. Bake in preheated oven for 20 to 25 minutes or until tops are golden brown and a toothpick inserted in the center comes out clean. Let cool in pan on a wire rack for 5 minutes, then transfer to the rack to cool.

Coconut Almond Joyful Muffins

Makes 12 muffins

Based on one of my favorite candy bars, this decadent coffee-cake-like treat is terrific for a coffee break, afternoon tea or brunch.

> **Tip:** If vegan chocolate chips are hard to come by, substitute $4\frac{1}{2}$ oz (135 g) vegan semisweet chocolate, chopped.

- Preheat oven to 375°F (190°C)
- 12-cup muffin pan, lined with paper liners

2 cups	all-purpose flour	500 mL
$2\frac{1}{2}$ tsp	baking powder	12 mL
$\frac{1}{2}$ tsp	salt	2 mL
$\frac{3}{4}$ cup	vegan granulated sugar or evaporated cane juice	175 mL
$\frac{1}{3}$ cup	coconut oil, warmed, or vegetable oil	75 mL
$\frac{3}{4}$ tsp	almond extract	3 mL
1 cup	vanilla-flavored soy yogurt	250 mL
1 cup	sweetened flaked or shredded coconut	250 mL
$\frac{3}{4}$ cup	vegan semisweet chocolate chips	175 mL
$\frac{1}{2}$ cup	sliced almonds	125 mL

1. In a large bowl, whisk together flour, baking powder and salt.

2. In a medium bowl, whisk together sugar, oil and almond extract until well blended. Whisk in yogurt.

3. Add the yogurt mixture to the flour mixture and stir until just blended. Gently fold in coconut and chocolate chips.

4. Divide batter equally among prepared muffin cups. Sprinkle with almonds.

5. Bake in preheated oven for 18 to 21 minutes or until tops are golden and a toothpick inserted in the center comes out clean. Let cool in pan on a wire rack for 5 minutes, then transfer to the rack to cool.

Cashew Butterscotch Muffins

Makes 12 muffins

I don't know anyone who dislikes butterscotch; I do know that these muffins are off the charts. The combination of salty (from the cashews) and sweet (toffee and brown sugar) is utterly irresistible.

- Preheat oven to 350°F (180°C)
- 12-cup muffin pan, lined with paper liners

1 1/2 cups	all-purpose flour	375 mL
3/4 tsp	baking powder	3 mL
3/4 tsp	baking soda	3 mL
1/4 tsp	salt	1 mL
2/3 cup	packed vegan dark brown sugar or Sucanat	150 mL
1/3 cup	vegan margarine, melted	75 mL
1 tsp	vanilla extract	5 mL
3/4 cup	vanilla-flavored soy yogurt	175 mL
1/3 cup	non-dairy milk (soy, almond, rice, hemp)	75 mL
1 cup	lightly salted roasted cashews, coarsely chopped	250 mL
3 tbsp	packed vegan dark brown sugar or Sucanat	45 mL

1. In a large bowl, whisk together flour, baking powder, baking soda and salt.

2. In a medium bowl, whisk together 2/3 cup (150 mL) brown sugar, margarine and vanilla until well blended. Whisk in yogurt and milk.

3. Add the yogurt mixture to the flour mixture and stir until just blended. Gently fold in cashews.

4. Divide batter equally among prepared muffin cups. Sprinkle muffin tops with 3 tbsp (45 mL) brown sugar.

5. Bake in preheated oven for 18 to 22 minutes or until tops are golden and a toothpick inserted in the center comes out clean. Let cool in pan on a wire rack for 3 minutes, then transfer to the rack to cool.

Brown Sugar Pecan Muffins

Makes 12 muffins

While these muffins appear modest, their nutty caramel flavor will draw everyone back for seconds and even thirds. Soy yogurt lends a subtle tang and extra tenderness to the overall texture.

- Preheat oven to 400°F (200°C)
- 12-cup muffin pan, greased

2 cups	all-purpose flour	500 mL
2 tsp	baking powder	10 mL
1/2 tsp	baking soda	2 mL
1/2 tsp	salt	2 mL
3/4 cup	packed vegan dark brown sugar or Sucanat, divided	175 mL
3/4 cup	plain non-dairy milk (soy, almond, rice, hemp)	175 mL
3/4 cup	plain soy yogurt	175 mL
1/3 cup	vegetable oil	75 mL
1 tsp	vanilla extract	5 mL
1 cup	chopped pecans, toasted	250 mL

1. In a large bowl, whisk together flour, baking powder, baking soda and salt.

2. In a medium bowl, whisk together 1/2 cup (125 mL) of the brown sugar, milk, yogurt, oil and vanilla until well blended.

3. Add the milk mixture to the flour mixture and stir until just blended. Gently fold in pecans.

4. Divide batter equally among prepared muffin cups. Sprinkle with the remaining brown sugar.

5. Bake in preheated oven for 18 to 22 minutes or until tops are golden brown and a toothpick inserted in the center comes out clean. Let cool in pan on a wire rack for 3 minutes, then transfer to the rack to cool.

Peanut Butter and Jelly Muffins

Finally, PB&J in one neat package. In this whimsical muffin, a peanut butter batter is filled with a spoonful of strawberry jam before heading off to the oven.

Tip: An equal amount of any other nut or seed butter (such as almond, cashew or sunflower seed) may be used in place of the peanut butter.

- Preheat oven to 350°F (180°C)
- Two 12-cup muffin pans, 16 cups greased

1 cup	all-purpose flour	250 mL
1/2 cup	whole wheat flour	125 mL
3/4 cup	large-flake (old-fashioned) rolled oats	75 mL
2 1/4 tsp	baking powder	11 mL
1 1/2 tsp	baking soda	7 mL
3/4 tsp	salt	3 mL
3/4 cup	plain non-dairy milk (soy, almond, rice, hemp)	175 mL
1/2 cup	brown rice syrup or agave nectar	125 mL
1/3 cup	vegetable oil	75 mL
3/4 cup	natural peanut butter, well stirred	175 mL
3/4 cup	mashed ripe bananas	175 mL
1 1/2 tbsp	cider vinegar	22 mL
1/2 cup	strawberry jam or preserves	125 mL

1. In a large bowl, whisk together all-purpose flour, whole wheat flour, oats, baking powder, baking soda and salt.

2. In a medium bowl, whisk together milk, syrup and oil until well blended. Whisk in peanut butter, bananas and vinegar until blended.

3. Add the peanut butter mixture to the flour mixture and stir until just blended.

4. Divide half the batter equally among prepared muffin cups. Spoon 2 tsp (10 mL) jam into the center of each cup. Top with the remaining batter.

5. Bake in preheated oven for 20 to 25 minutes or until tops are golden brown and firm to the touch. Let cool in pans on a wire rack for 5 minutes, then transfer to the rack to cool.

Candied Ginger Muffins

Makes 12 muffins

Ground ginger and crystallized ginger amp up the flavor of these muffins. Try serving them with fresh fruit, a delicious counterpoint to the peppery notes of the spice.

Tip: If you like the peppery kick of ginger, consider complementing it by adding ¼ tsp (1 mL) finely ground black pepper to the batter.

- Preheat oven to 400°F (200°C)
- 12-cup muffin pan, greased

1⅔ cups	all-purpose flour	400 mL
⅓ cup	whole wheat flour	75 mL
2½ tsp	ground ginger	12 mL
2 tsp	baking powder	10 mL
½ tsp	baking soda	2 mL
½ tsp	salt	2 mL
⅓ cup	packed vegan light brown sugar or Sucanat	75 mL
1 cup	plain soy yogurt	250 mL
½ cup	plain non-dairy milk (soy, almond, rice, hemp)	125 mL
⅓ cup	vegetable oil	75 mL
1 tsp	vanilla extract	5 mL
¼ cup	minced crystallized ginger	60 mL

1. In a large bowl, whisk together all-purpose flour, whole wheat flour, ground ginger, baking powder, baking soda and salt.

2. In a medium bowl, whisk together brown sugar, yogurt, milk, oil and vanilla until well blended.

3. Add the yogurt mixture to the flour mixture and stir until just blended. Gently fold in crystallized ginger.

4. Divide batter equally among prepared muffin cups.

5. Bake in preheated oven for 18 to 22 minutes or until tops are golden brown and a toothpick inserted in the center comes out clean. Let cool in pan on a wire rack for 3 minutes, then transfer to the rack to cool.

Chai Latte Muffins

Makes 12 muffins

Scented with many of the spices of chai, these muffins are wonderful with hot black tea.

> **Tip:** As wonderful as these muffins are for teatime, they are easily transformed into hearty morning muffins by substituting 1 cup (250 mL) whole wheat flour for half the all-purpose flour.

- 12-cup muffin pan, greased

1 cup	vanilla-flavored non-dairy milk (soy, almond, rice, hemp)	250 mL
2 tbsp	loose black tea	30 mL
2 cups	all-purpose flour	500 mL
2 tsp	baking powder	10 mL
1 1/2 tsp	ground cinnamon	7 mL
1 1/2 tsp	ground cardamom	7 mL
1/2 tsp	ground ginger	2 mL
1/2 tsp	baking soda	2 mL
1/2 tsp	salt	2 mL
1/4 tsp	ground cloves	1 mL
2/3 cup	packed vegan light brown sugar or Sucanat	150 mL
2/3 cup	plain soy yogurt	150 mL
1/3 cup	vegetable oil	75 mL
1 tsp	vanilla extract	5 mL

1. In a small saucepan, bring milk and tea to a simmer over medium heat. Remove from heat, cover and let steep for 10 minutes. Strain through a fine-mesh sieve into a medium bowl, discarding tea leaves, and let cool.

2. Preheat oven to 400°F (200°C).

3. In a large bowl, whisk together flour, baking powder, cinnamon, cardamom, ginger, baking soda, salt and cloves.

4. Whisk brown sugar, yogurt, oil and vanilla into milk mixture until well blended.

5. Add the yogurt mixture to the flour mixture and stir until just blended.

6. Divide batter equally among prepared muffin cups.

7. Bake for 19 to 23 minutes or until tops are golden brown and a toothpick inserted in the center comes out clean. Let cool in pan on a wire rack for 5 minutes, then transfer to the rack to cool.

Mocha Muffins

Makes 12 muffins

Cocoa-cinnamon batter, chocolate chips and a shot of espresso add up to a handful of heaven for java junkies.

Tip: If you love the flavor of coffee but not the caffeine, substitute 1 1/2 tbsp (22 mL) decaffeinated instant coffee powder for the espresso powder.

- Preheat oven to 375°F (190°C)
- 12-cup muffin pan, greased

2 cups	all-purpose flour	500 mL
1/4 cup	unsweetened cocoa powder (not Dutch process)	60 mL
2 1/2 tsp	baking powder	12 mL
1/2 tsp	salt	2 mL
1/4 tsp	baking soda	1 mL
1/4 tsp	ground cinnamon	1 mL
3/4 cup	vegan granulated sugar or evaporated cane juice	175 mL
3/4 cup	vanilla-flavored soy yogurt	175 mL
1/2 cup	plain non-dairy milk (soy, almond, rice, hemp)	125 mL
1/2 cup	vegetable oil	125 mL
1 tbsp	instant espresso powder	15 mL
1/2 cup	vegan miniature semisweet chocolate chips	125 mL

1. In a large bowl, whisk together flour, cocoa powder, baking powder, salt, baking soda and cinnamon.

2. In a medium bowl, whisk together sugar, yogurt, milk, oil and espresso powder until well blended.

3. Add the yogurt mixture to the flour mixture and stir until just blended. Gently fold in chocolate chips.

4. Divide batter equally among prepared muffin cups.

5. Bake in preheated oven for 18 to 22 minutes or until a toothpick inserted in the center comes out clean. Let cool in pan on a wire rack for 5 minutes, then transfer to the rack to cool.

Chocolate Chip Cookie Muffins

Makes 12 muffins

If you think the idea of chocolate chip cookies for breakfast is brilliant, these muffins are for you. They have the advantage of being more healthful than cookies, much less sweet and filling enough to propel you through the morning.

- Preheat oven to 400°F (200°C)
- 12-cup muffin pan, greased

1 1/2 cups	all-purpose flour	375 mL
1/2 cup	whole wheat flour	125 mL
2 tsp	baking powder	10 mL
1/2 tsp	baking soda	2 mL
1/2 tsp	salt	2 mL
1/4 tsp	ground cinnamon	1 mL
1/3 cup	packed vegan light brown sugar or Sucanat	75 mL
2/3 cup	plain non-dairy milk (soy, almond, rice, hemp)	150 mL
2/3 cup	plain soy yogurt	150 mL
1/2 cup	vegan margarine, melted	125 mL
1 tsp	vanilla extract	5 mL
3/4 cup	vegan miniature semisweet chocolate chips	175 mL

1. In a large bowl, whisk together all-purpose flour, whole wheat flour, baking powder, baking soda, salt and cinnamon.

2. In a medium bowl, whisk together brown sugar, milk, yogurt, margarine and vanilla until blended.

3. Add the yogurt mixture to the flour mixture and stir until just blended. Gently fold in chocolate chips.

4. Divide batter equally among prepared muffin cups.

5. Bake in preheated oven for 18 to 22 minutes or until tops are golden brown and a toothpick inserted in the center comes out clean. Let cool in pan on a wire rack for 5 minutes, then transfer to the rack to cool.

Chocolate Chip Coffee Cake Muffins

Makes 12 muffins

Friends and family will be throwing off the covers to ensure they get up in time for more than one of these muffins. Be sure to tuck one or more away for your afternoon coffee break.

> **Tip:** For more delicately textured muffins, substitute all-purpose flour for the whole wheat pastry flour.

- Preheat oven to 350°F (180°C)
- 12-cup muffin pan, greased

Topping

½ cup	whole wheat pastry flour	125 mL
½ cup	firmly packed light brown sugar	125 mL
½ tsp	ground cinnamon	2 mL
¼ cup	vegan margarine, melted	60 mL

Muffins

2 cups	whole wheat pastry flour	500 mL
2½ tsp	baking powder	12 mL
1 tsp	ground cinnamon	5 mL
½ tsp	baking soda	2 mL
½ tsp	salt	2 mL
¾ cup	vegan granulated sugar or evaporated cane juice	175 mL
¾ cup	vanilla-flavored soy yogurt	175 mL
⅔ cup	vanilla-flavored non-dairy milk (soy, almond, rice, hemp)	150 mL
½ cup	vegetable oil	125 mL
1 tsp	vanilla extract	5 mL
⅔ cup	vegan miniature semisweet chocolate chips	150 mL

1. *Topping:* In a small bowl, combine flour, brown sugar and cinnamon. Add margarine, tossing with a fork until mixture is crumbly. Refrigerate until ready to use.

2. *Muffins:* In a large bowl, whisk together flour, baking powder, cinnamon, baking soda and salt.

3. In a medium bowl, whisk together sugar, yogurt, milk, oil and vanilla until well blended.

Tip: To increase the chocolate decadence of these muffins, add $1/4$ cup (60 mL) vegan miniature semisweet chocolate chips to the completed topping mixture.

4. Add the yogurt mixture to the flour mixture and stir until just blended. Gently fold in chocolate chips.

5. Divide batter equally among prepared muffin cups. Sprinkle with topping.

6. Bake in preheated oven for 20 to 25 minutes or until tops are golden and a toothpick inserted in the center comes out clean. Let cool in pan on a wire rack for 5 minutes, then transfer to the rack to cool.

Peppermint Chocolate Chunk Muffins

Makes 12 muffins

In these festive treats, the muffin base is infused with peppermint flavor and flecked with chunks of bittersweet chocolate. A sprinkling of red-and-white peppermint candies on top makes for a fun presentation.

- Preheat oven to 375°F (190°C)
- 12-cup muffin pan, lined with paper liners

2 cups	all-purpose flour	500 mL
2 tsp	baking powder	10 mL
1/2 tsp	baking soda	2 mL
1/2 tsp	salt	2 mL
3/4 cup	vegan granulated sugar or evaporated cane juice	175 mL
3/4 cup	vanilla-flavored soy yogurt	175 mL
1/2 cup	non-dairy milk (soy, almond, rice, hemp)	125 mL
1/3 cup	vegan margarine, melted	75 mL
1 tsp	peppermint extract	5 mL
6 oz	vegan bittersweet chocolate, chopped into chunks	175 g
1/3 cup	coarsely crushed red-and-white-striped peppermint candies	75 mL

1. In a large bowl, whisk together flour, baking powder, baking soda and salt.

2. In a medium bowl, whisk together sugar, yogurt, milk, margarine and peppermint extract until well blended.

3. Add the yogurt mixture to the flour mixture and stir until just blended. Gently fold in chocolate.

4. Divide batter equally among prepared muffin cups. Sprinkle with candies.

5. Bake in preheated oven for 18 to 22 minutes or until tops are golden and a toothpick inserted in the center comes out clean. Let cool in pan on a wire rack for 3 minutes, then transfer to the rack to cool.

Lunch and Supper Muffins

Whole Wheat Biscuit Muffins

Makes 12 muffins

This whole wheat version of basic biscuits is made even easier by the use of a muffin pan. They are deliciously wheaty and substantial. A little bit of all-purpose flour in the batter keeps the muffins light in texture, while the non-dairy milk and margarine keep them soft.

Tip: When baking with vegan margarine, avoid tub margarine and use stick margarine. Tub margarine contains extra water, for easier spreadability. This is great for toast, but can negatively affect vegan baked goods due to its lower fat content and higher water content. Stick margarine still contains more water than butter in most cases, but will perform better than tub margarine.

- Preheat oven to 400°F (200°C)
- 12-cup muffin pan, greased

1½ cups	whole wheat pastry flour	375 mL
1 cup	all-purpose flour	250 mL
4 tsp	baking powder	20 mL
¾ tsp	salt	3 mL
¾ cup	cold vegan stick margarine, cut into ¼-inch pieces	175 mL
¾ cup	plain non-dairy milk (soy, almond, rice, hemp)	175 mL

1. In a large bowl, whisk together whole wheat pastry flour, all-purpose flour, baking powder and salt. Using a pastry cutter or your fingers, cut or rub in margarine until mixture resembles coarse crumbs. Stir in milk until just moistened.

2. Divide batter equally among prepared muffin cups.

3. Bake in preheated oven for 16 to 19 minutes or until tops are golden and a toothpick inserted in the center comes out clean. Let cool in pan on a wire rack for 3 minutes, then transfer to the rack to cool.

Oat, Wheat and Spelt Supper Muffins

Makes 12 muffins

The humble list of ingredients here belies the great flavor of these muffins. Use leftovers to make a quick sandwich with some roasted vegetables, fresh greens or sliced seitan.

Tip: Spelt flour has a higher protein content than other types of grain and flour, making it a great choice for vegans. Either whole-grain or white spelt flour can be used in this muffin recipe, but whole-grain spelt flour is the more nutritious option, as it contains a heftier portion of protein and dietary fiber.

- Preheat oven to 350°F (180°C)
- 12-cup muffin pan, greased

1½ cups	non-dairy milk (soy, almond, rice, hemp)	375 mL
1 tbsp	cider vinegar	15 mL
1 cup	large-flake (old-fashioned) rolled oats	250 mL
½ cup	spelt flour	125 mL
½ cup	whole wheat flour	125 mL
1 tsp	baking soda	5 mL
¼ tsp	salt	1 mL
¼ tsp	freshly ground black pepper	1 mL
¼ cup	dark (cooking) molasses	60 mL
¼ cup	olive oil or vegetable oil	60 mL

1. In a glass measuring cup, combine milk and vinegar. Let stand for 5 minutes.

2. In a large bowl, whisk together oats, spelt flour, whole wheat flour, baking soda, salt and pepper.

3. In a medium bowl, whisk together molasses and oil until well blended. Whisk in milk mixture until blended.

4. Add the milk mixture to the flour mixture and stir until just blended.

5. Divide batter equally among prepared muffin cups.

6. Bake in preheated oven for 20 to 25 minutes or until tops are golden and a toothpick inserted in the center comes out clean. Let cool in pan on a wire rack for 3 minutes, then transfer to the rack to cool.

Boston Brown Bread Muffins

Makes 12 muffins

Boston brown bread is a nostalgic favorite — my parents would buy cans of it to keep on hand for quick vegetarian lunches (they always partnered it with baked beans) for me and my siblings. I can attest that this muffin interpretation hits all the right notes.

> **Tip:** Before measuring sticky ingredients like maple syrup, molasses or honey, coat the inside of your measuring cup with nonstick cooking spray or a bit of oil. The sticky liquid will slide out and leave a perfectly empty measuring cup.

- Preheat oven to 400°F (200°C)
- 12-cup muffin pan, greased

1 cup	whole wheat flour	250 mL
1/2 cup	yellow cornmeal	125 mL
1 1/2 tsp	baking soda	7 mL
3/4 tsp	salt	3 mL
1/3 cup	packed vegan dark brown sugar or Sucanat	75 mL
3/4 cup	plain soy yogurt	175 mL
1/2 cup	plain non-dairy milk (soy, almond, rice, hemp)	125 mL
1/3 cup	dark (cooking) molasses	75 mL
1/3 cup	vegetable oil	75 mL
1 cup	raisins	250 mL

1. In a large bowl, whisk together flour, cornmeal, baking soda and salt.

2. In a medium bowl, whisk together brown sugar, yogurt, milk, molasses and oil until well blended.

3. Add the yogurt mixture to the flour mixture and stir until just blended. Gently fold in raisins.

4. Divide batter equally among prepared muffin cups.

5. Bake in preheated oven for 14 to 17 minutes or until a toothpick inserted in the center comes out clean. Let cool in pan on a wire rack for 5 minutes, then transfer to the rack to cool.

Irish Brown Bread Muffins

Makes 12 muffins

With a hearty whole-grain flavor punctuated by sweet currants, these muffins are perfect at any meal of the day.

> **Tip:** No cooling rack? No problem. Before preheating the oven, transfer the lower oven rack to a countertop. It's perfect for cooling.

- Preheat oven to 425°F (220°C)
- 12-cup muffin pan, greased

1 cup	plain non-dairy milk (soy, almond, rice, hemp)	250 mL
1 tsp	cider vinegar	5 mL
2 tbsp	vegetable oil	30 mL
1½ cups	whole wheat flour	375 mL
½ cup	all-purpose flour	125 mL
¼ cup	quick-cooking rolled oats	60 mL
2 tbsp	vegan granulated sugar or evaporated cane juice	30 mL
1 tsp	baking soda	5 mL
½ tsp	salt	2 mL
½ cup	dried currants	125 mL

1. In a glass measuring cup, combine milk and vinegar. Let stand for 5 minutes or until curdled. Stir in oil.

2. In a large bowl, whisk together whole wheat flour, all-purpose flour, oats, sugar, baking soda and salt.

3. Add the milk mixture to the flour mixture and stir until just blended. Gently fold in currants.

4. Divide batter equally among prepared muffin cups.

5. Bake in preheated oven for 15 to 20 minutes or until tops sound hollow when tapped and a toothpick inserted in the center comes out clean. Let cool in pan on a wire rack for 3 minutes, then transfer to the rack to cool.

Pumpernickel Muffins

Makes 12 muffins

Dark and delicious, these muffins top my list as an accompaniment for homemade soup.

> **Tip:** Either light or dark rye flour can be used in this recipe, but dark rye is more traditional for pumpernickel bread. In addition, dark rye flour retains most of the bran and germ and provides magnesium, trace minerals, folate, thiamin and niacin. Rye flour retains more nutrients than wheat, due to the difficulty in separating the germ and bran from the endosperm of rye.

- Preheat oven to 375°F (190°C)
- 12-cup muffin pan, greased

1¼ cups	rye flour	300 mL
1¼ cups	all-purpose flour	300 mL
2 tsp	baking powder	10 mL
1 tsp	baking soda	5 mL
1 tsp	salt	5 mL
¾ cup	plain soy yogurt	175 mL
⅓ cup	plain non-dairy milk (soy, almond, rice, hemp)	75 mL
¼ cup	dark (cooking) molasses	60 mL
¼ cup	vegetable oil	60 mL
1½ tsp	instant espresso powder	7 mL
2 tbsp	caraway seeds (optional)	30 mL

1. In a large bowl, whisk together rye flour, all-purpose flour, baking powder, baking soda and salt.

2. In a medium bowl, whisk together yogurt, milk, molasses, oil and espresso powder until well blended.

3. Add the yogurt mixture to the flour mixture and stir until just blended.

4. Divide batter equally among prepared muffin cups. Sprinkle with caraway seeds (if using).

5. Bake in preheated oven for 20 to 25 minutes or until a toothpick inserted in the center comes out clean. Let cool in pan on a wire rack for 5 minutes, then transfer to the rack. Serve warm or let cool.

Herbed Rye Muffins

Makes 12 muffins

In this easy and hugely versatile recipe, fresh herbs and rye flour are transformed into a boast-worthy muffin. And because you can vary the herbs by season — or even use dried herbs — they are muffins to be enjoyed year-round.

- Preheat oven to 375°F (190°C)
- 12-cup muffin pan, greased

1¼ cups	rye flour	300 mL
½ cup	brown rice flour	125 mL
4 tsp	baking powder	20 mL
¾ tsp	salt	3 mL
¾ cup	plain non-dairy milk (soy, almond, rice, hemp)	175 mL
¼ cup	vegetable oil	60 mL
3 tbsp	brown rice syrup	45 mL
2 tbsp	minced fresh chives	30 mL
1 tbsp	minced fresh dill	15 mL

1. In a large bowl, whisk together rye flour, brown rice flour, baking powder and salt.

2. In a medium bowl, whisk together milk, oil and syrup until well blended.

3. Add the milk mixture to the flour mixture and stir until just blended. Gently fold in chives and dill.

4. Divide batter equally among prepared muffin cups.

5. Bake in preheated oven for 22 to 26 minutes or until tops are golden brown and a toothpick inserted in the center comes out clean. Let cool in pan on a wire rack for 5 minutes, then transfer to the rack to cool.

NYC Onion Rye Muffins

Makes 16 muffins

I know I am setting myself up for critique with the name I've chosen for these muffins, but I have had my share of New York City onion rye bread, and these muffins are worthy of their eponym. They are simple to make, but that's not the point here — deliciousness is, and that's where this recipe shines.

- Preheat oven to 375°F (190°C)
- Two 12-cup muffin pans, 16 cups greased

1²⁄₃ cups	non-dairy milk (soy, almond, rice, hemp)	400 mL
1¹⁄₂ tbsp	cider vinegar	22 mL
2 cups	all-purpose flour	500 mL
1 cup	rye flour	250 mL
2 tbsp	caraway seeds	30 mL
1¹⁄₂ tsp	salt	7 mL
1 tsp	baking soda	5 mL
²⁄₃ cup	minced onion	150 mL
2 tbsp	vegan granulated sugar or evaporated cane juice	30 mL
¹⁄₄ cup	vegan margarine, melted	60 mL
1 tbsp	yellow cornmeal	15 mL

1. In a glass measuring cup, combine milk and vinegar. Let stand for 5 minutes.

2. In a large bowl, whisk together all-purpose flour, rye flour, caraway seeds, salt and baking soda.

3. In a medium bowl, whisk together onion, sugar and margarine until well blended. Whisk in milk mixture until blended.

4. Add the milk mixture to the flour mixture and stir until just blended.

5. Sprinkle cornmeal into prepared muffin cups, shaking to coat bottom and sides, then shake out excess. Divide batter equally among cups.

6. Bake in preheated oven for 20 to 25 minutes or until tops are golden and a toothpick inserted in the center comes out clean. Let cool in pans on a wire rack for 5 minutes, then transfer to the rack. Serve warm or let cool completely.

Rosemary Muffins

Makes 12 muffins

The perfect soup partner, these fragrant muffins are as impressive and delicious as they are easy to make.

Tip: Use a sharp knife when chopping rosemary. A dull knife will bruise the leaves and make them taste bitter. A clean cut releases just the right amount of the potent oils.

- Preheat oven to 375°F (190°C)
- Blender
- 12-cup muffin pan, greased

1½ cups	all-purpose flour	375 mL
¾ cup	whole wheat flour	175 mL
1 tbsp	vegan granulated sugar or evaporated cane juice	15 mL
2½ tsp	baking powder	12 mL
2 tsp	minced fresh rosemary	10 mL
½ tsp	salt	2 mL
⅛ tsp	freshly ground black pepper	0.5 mL
¼ cup	ground flax seeds	60 mL
1 cup	plain non-dairy milk (soy, almond, rice, hemp)	250 mL
¼ cup	vegetable oil	60 mL

1. In a large bowl, whisk together all-purpose flour, whole wheat flour, sugar, baking powder, rosemary, salt and pepper.

2. In blender, process flax seeds and ½ cup (125 mL) water for 1 minute or until thickened and frothy. Add milk and oil; process for 30 seconds or until combined.

3. Add the milk mixture to the flour mixture and stir until just blended.

4. Divide batter equally among prepared muffin cups.

5. Bake in preheated oven for 20 to 24 minutes or until tops are golden brown and a toothpick inserted in the center comes out clean. Let cool in pan on a wire rack for 3 minutes, then transfer to the rack to cool.

Fresh Corn and Thyme Muffins

Makes 12 muffins

When you've had your fill of fresh corn on the cob, shuck the rest and cut off the kernels for these excellent muffins. Serve them warm, with a pat of vegan margarine, at your next barbecue. And who could say no to a leftover muffin, toasted and topped with a juicy slice of ripe tomato?

Tip: If you don't have fresh thyme on hand, you can use 1½ tsp (7 mL) dried thyme instead.

- Preheat oven to 400°F (200°C)
- 12-cup muffin pan, greased

1⅓ cups	non-dairy milk (soy, almond, rice, hemp)	325 mL
1 tbsp	cider vinegar	15 mL
2 cups	all-purpose flour	500 mL
1¼ tsp	baking soda	6 mL
¼ tsp	salt	1 mL
¼ tsp	freshly ground black pepper	1 mL
1 tbsp	vegan granulated sugar or evaporated cane juice	15 mL
¼ cup	olive oil or vegetable oil	60 mL
1½ cups	fresh or frozen (thawed) corn kernels	375 mL
1 tbsp	minced fresh thyme	15 mL

1. In a glass measuring cup, combine milk and vinegar. Let stand for 5 minutes.

2. In a large bowl, whisk together flour, baking soda, salt and pepper.

3. In a medium bowl, whisk together sugar and oil until well blended. Whisk in milk mixture until blended. Stir in corn and thyme.

4. Add the milk mixture to the flour mixture and stir until just blended.

5. Divide batter equally among prepared muffin cups.

6. Bake in preheated oven for 19 to 22 minutes or until tops are golden and a toothpick inserted in the center comes out clean. Let cool in pan on a wire rack for 3 minutes, then transfer to the rack. Serve warm or let cool.

Jalapeño Corn Muffins

Makes 12 muffins

I'm at the point where I won't even consider eating my black bean chili without baking a batch of these muffins. They have just the right amount of heat, plus a bit of smoky flavor.

- Preheat oven to 375°F (190°C)
- 12-cup muffin pan, greased

1 cup	all-purpose flour	250 mL
1 cup	yellow cornmeal, preferably stone-ground	250 mL
1 tbsp	baking powder	15 mL
1 tsp	ground cumin	5 mL
¾ tsp	salt	3 mL
3 tbsp	vegan granulated sugar or evaporated cane juice	45 mL
¾ cup	plain soy yogurt	175 mL
⅓ cup	plain non-dairy milk (soy, almond, rice, hemp)	75 mL
⅓ cup	vegetable oil	75 mL
1 cup	fresh or frozen (thawed) corn kernels	75 mL
2 tsp	minced seeded jalapeño pepper	10 mL

1. In a large bowl, whisk together flour, cornmeal, baking powder, cumin and salt.

2. In a medium bowl, whisk together sugar, yogurt, milk and oil until well blended.

3. Add the yogurt mixture to the flour mixture and stir until just blended. Gently fold in corn and jalapeño.

4. Divide batter equally among prepared muffin cups.

5. Bake in preheated oven for 16 to 19 minutes or until tops are golden and a toothpick inserted in the center comes out clean. Let cool in pan on a wire rack for 10 minutes, then transfer to the rack. Serve warm or let cool.

Parsley Lemon Muffins

Makes 10 muffins

One of the things I love about both parsley and lemon is their versatility. Here they shine in shades of white, green and gold without missing a beat.

Tip: To keep fresh parsley on hand for an impromptu batch of these muffins, try freezing it. Wash and dry the parsley, then chop the leaves in a food processor. Place the chopped parsley in a plastic freezer bag, roll up the bag to remove all the air and stick it in the freezer. It will keep for up to 6 months. The frozen parsley will thaw at room temperature in a matter of minutes.

- Preheat oven to 400°F (200°C)
- 12-cup muffin pan, 10 cups greased

1 cup	non-dairy milk (soy, almond, rice, hemp)	250 mL
2 tsp	grated lemon zest	10 mL
2 tbsp	freshly squeezed lemon juice	30 mL
¾ cup	fresh parsley leaves, chopped	175 mL
⅓ cup	olive oil	75 mL
1¾ cups	all-purpose flour	425 mL
2 tsp	baking powder	10 mL
½ tsp	baking soda	2 mL
¼ tsp	salt	1 mL
⅛ tsp	freshly ground black pepper	0.5 mL
2 tbsp	sesame seeds (optional)	30 mL

1. In a glass measuring cup, combine milk, lemon zest and lemon juice. Let stand for 5 minutes, then whisk in parsley and oil.

2. In a large bowl, whisk together flour, baking powder, baking soda, salt and pepper.

3. Add the milk mixture to the flour mixture and stir until just blended.

4. Divide batter equally among prepared muffin cups. Sprinkle with sesame seeds (if using).

5. Bake in preheated oven for 20 to 22 minutes or until tops are golden and a toothpick inserted in the center comes out clean. Let cool in pan on a wire rack for 5 minutes, then transfer to the rack to cool.

Spinach Basil Muffins

Makes 18 muffins

Here, I've pepped up my fail-safe savory muffin with a combination of spinach, basil and garlic.

> **Tip:** When measuring lots of cups, tablespoons or teaspoons in succession, make it a habit to count out loud as you add to the bowl. It may make you feel silly, but not as much as if you add double the amount of baking soda to the batter and ruin your muffins!

- Preheat oven to 400°F (200°C)
- Two 12-cup muffin pans, 18 cups greased

3 cups	all-purpose flour	750 mL
1 tbsp	baking powder	15 mL
1 tbsp	dried basil	15 mL
1 tsp	garlic powder	5 mL
1 1/4 tsp	salt	6 mL
1/2 tsp	baking soda	2 mL
3/4 cup	plain non-dairy milk (soy, almond, rice, hemp)	175 mL
3/4 cup	plain soy yogurt	175 mL
1/2 cup	vegetable oil	125 mL
1	package (10 oz/300 g) frozen chopped spinach, thawed and squeezed dry	1

1. In a large bowl, whisk together flour, baking powder, basil, garlic powder, salt and baking soda.

2. In a medium bowl, whisk together milk, yogurt and oil until well blended. Stir in spinach until blended.

3. Add the spinach mixture to the flour mixture and stir until just blended.

4. Divide batter equally among prepared muffin cups.

5. Bake in preheated oven for 18 to 22 minutes or until tops are golden and a toothpick inserted in the center comes out clean. Let cool in pans on a wire rack for 3 minutes, then transfer to the rack. Serve warm or let cool.

Kale and Toasted Walnut Muffins

Makes 12 muffins

When my husband and I were in graduate school, Saturday morning trips to the farmers' market in Bloomington, Indiana, were a regular feature of our weekends. During the early summer months, though, he would grumble that it wasn't worth the trip when kale and turnips were the predominant offerings. His perspective was somewhat skewed — he overlooked the honey and flowers — but there really was a plethora of kale and turnips. Somewhere along the way, I developed these muffins to use up some of the kale bounty. The cooked kale is fantastic with the nutty whole wheat batter and toasted walnuts.

- Preheat oven to 375°F (190°C)
- 12-cup muffin pan, greased

1 cup	whole wheat flour	250 mL
1 cup	all-purpose flour	250 mL
1 tbsp	baking powder	15 mL
1 tsp	salt	5 mL
1/4 tsp	baking soda	1 mL
1 1/4 cups	non-dairy milk (soy, almond, rice, hemp)	300 mL
1/4 cup	olive oil	60 mL
1 tbsp	brown rice syrup	15 mL
2/3 cup	chopped drained cooked kale	150 mL
3/4 cup	chopped walnuts, toasted	175 mL

1. In a large bowl, whisk together whole wheat flour, all-purpose flour, baking powder, salt and baking soda.

2. In a medium bowl, whisk together milk, oil and syrup until well blended. Stir in kale and walnuts.

3. Add the milk mixture to the flour mixture and stir until just blended.

4. Divide batter equally among prepared muffin cups.

5. Bake in preheated oven for 21 to 26 minutes or until tops are golden and a toothpick inserted in the center comes out clean. Let cool in pan on a wire rack for 3 minutes, then transfer to the rack to cool.

> **Tip:** Kale has a mild cabbage flavor and is a nutritional powerhouse. Look for dark green, frilly leaves that are free of any yellowing or wilting (signs of age). If the center stalks are thicker than a pencil, remove and discard them before cooking.
>
> For 2/3 cup (150 mL) chopped drained cooked kale, you'll need about 3 cups (750 mL) packed kale leaves. I just chop it and sauté it in a little olive oil until it's completely wilted.

Fresh Broccoli Muffins

Makes 12 muffins

Deep-colored broccoli seems like something new in these rich, satisfying muffins, enhanced with green onions and a hint of Dijon mustard.

Tip: When purchasing broccoli, look for compact, tightly closed florets and thin-skinned stems that are on the slender side. Avoid broccoli that is dried or cracked on the cut end or that has obviously woody stems, and leave behind any yellowing specimens. If it passes the visual inspection, take a whiff: broccoli should smell fresh, not strong and cabbage-like. Store it in a loose (unsealed) plastic bag in the refrigerator crisper. It will keep for a few days, but you should use it as quickly as possible, before the florets start to deteriorate.

- Preheat oven to 400°F (200°C)
- 12-cup muffin pan, lined with paper liners

1¾ cups	all-purpose flour	425 mL
1 cup	quick-cooking rolled oats	250 mL
2¼ tsp	baking powder	11 mL
2 tsp	vegan granulated sugar or evaporated cane juice	10 mL
½ tsp	salt	2 mL
1¼ cups	non-dairy milk (soy, almond, rice, hemp)	300 mL
¼ cup	olive oil	60 mL
2 tsp	Dijon mustard	10 mL
1 cup	finely chopped broccoli	250 mL
¾ cup	chopped green onions (scallions)	175 mL
1 cup	shredded vegan Cheddar-style cheese alternative (optional)	250 mL

1. In a large bowl, whisk together flour, oats, baking powder, sugar and salt.

2. In a medium bowl, whisk together milk, oil and mustard until well blended. Stir in broccoli, green onions and cheese (if using).

3. Add the broccoli mixture to the flour mixture and stir until just blended.

4. Divide batter equally among prepared muffin cups.

5. Bake in preheated oven for 18 to 22 minutes or until a toothpick inserted in the center comes out clean. Let cool in pan on a wire rack for 5 minutes, then transfer to the rack. Serve warm or let cool.

Whole Wheat Mushroom Muffins

Makes 12 muffins

I like to serve these earthy muffins with ratatouille or vegetable soup for a light, quick, nutritious meal. Mushrooms are particularly high in selenium, which is thought to fight against several forms of cancer. They are also an excellent source of potassium and a good source of three essential B vitamins: niacin, riboflavin and pantothenic acid.

> **Tip:** Choose mushrooms that are firm and slightly moist, with no signs of decay. They should have a woodsy scent and look fresh and alive. The best ones will feel heavy for their size. Warm air and water cause mushrooms to decay, so keep them cool and dry. Store your mushrooms in a basket or an open paper bag in the refrigerator, and don't wash them.

- 12-cup muffin pan, greased

1/3 cup	olive oil, divided	75 mL
8 oz	fresh cremini or button mushrooms, chopped	250 g
	Salt and freshly ground black pepper	
1 1/2 cups	non-dairy milk (soy, almond, rice, hemp)	375 mL
1 tbsp	cider vinegar	15 mL
2 cups	whole wheat pastry flour	500 mL
2 1/4 tsp	baking powder	11 mL
1 tsp	dried thyme	5 mL
1/2 tsp	baking soda	2 mL
1/2 cup	chopped walnuts, toasted	125 mL

1. In a large nonstick skillet, heat 1 tbsp (15 mL) of the oil over medium heat. Add mushrooms and cook, stirring, for about 10 minutes or until tender and liquid has evaporated. Season to taste with salt and pepper. Remove from heat and let cool.

2. Preheat oven to 375°F (190°C).

3. In a glass measuring cup, combine milk and vinegar. Let stand for 5 minutes.

4. In a large bowl, whisk together flour, baking powder, thyme, baking soda, 1/2 tsp (2 mL) salt and 1/8 tsp (0.5 mL) pepper.

5. Whisk the remaining oil into the milk mixture until well blended. Add the milk mixture to the flour mixture and stir until just blended. Gently fold in mushroom mixture and walnuts.

6. Divide batter equally among prepared muffin cups.

7. Bake for 20 to 25 minutes or until a toothpick inserted in the center comes out clean. Let cool in pan on a wire rack for 3 minutes, then transfer to the rack to cool slightly. Serve warm.

Green Onion Muffins

Makes 12 muffins

These muffins are a pretty and scrumptious way to showcase humble, yet delicately delicious, fresh green onions.

> **Tip:** Be sure to store green onions away from odor-sensitive foods such as mushrooms and corn, which can absorb their odor.

- Preheat oven to 400°F (200°C)
- 12-cup muffin pan, lined with paper liners

¾ cup	all-purpose flour	175 mL
¾ cup	whole wheat flour	175 mL
1 tbsp	baking powder	15 mL
½ tsp	salt	2 mL
2 tsp	vegan granulated sugar or evaporated cane juice	10 mL
1 cup	non-dairy milk (soy, almond, rice, hemp)	250 mL
⅓ cup	vegan margarine, melted	75 mL
1 cup	chopped green onions (scallions)	250 mL

1. In a large bowl, whisk together all-purpose flour, whole wheat flour, baking powder and salt.

2. In a medium bowl, whisk together sugar, milk and margarine until well blended. Stir in green onions.

3. Add the milk mixture to the flour mixture and stir until just blended.

4. Divide batter equally among prepared muffin cups.

5. Bake in preheated oven for 18 to 22 minutes or until tops are golden and a toothpick inserted in the center comes out clean. Let cool in pan on a wire rack for 5 minutes, then transfer to the rack to cool.

Sesame Scallion Muffins

Makes 12 muffins

These muffins were inspired by the sesame-scallion pancakes at one of my favorite Chinese restaurants.

Tip: To prevent green onions from drying up in the refrigerator, store them in a glass of water. Simply remove any discolored outer layers and trim the green tops, but don't cut the roots. Stand the onions in a glass of water, cover the tops with a plastic bag and secure the bag with a rubber band. If you change the water occasionally, the onions will keep almost twice as long as if they were left in the produce crisper.

- Preheat oven to 400°F (200°C)
- 12-cup muffin pan, greased

1½ cups	all-purpose flour	375 mL
½ cup	whole wheat flour	125 mL
2¼ tsp	baking powder	11 mL
1 tsp	baking soda	5 mL
½ tsp	salt	2 mL
1 tbsp	vegan granulated sugar or evaporated cane juice	15 mL
¾ cup	plain non-dairy milk (soy, almond, rice, hemp)	175 mL
¾ cup	plain soy yogurt	175 mL
¼ cup	vegetable oil	60 mL
2 tbsp	toasted sesame oil	30 mL
1 cup	chopped green onions (scallions)	250 mL
2 tbsp	sesame seeds	30 mL

1. In a large bowl, whisk together all-purpose flour, whole wheat flour, baking powder, baking soda and salt.

2. In a medium bowl, whisk together sugar, milk, yogurt, vegetable oil and sesame oil until well blended.

3. Add the milk mixture to the flour mixture and stir until just blended. Gently fold in green onions.

4. Divide batter equally among prepared muffin cups. Sprinkle with sesame seeds.

5. Bake in preheated oven for 18 to 22 minutes or until tops are golden brown and a toothpick inserted in the center comes out clean. Let cool in pan on a wire rack for 3 minutes, then transfer to the rack. Serve warm or let cool.

Scallion, Cranberry and Horseradish Muffins

Makes 12 muffins

Here, the tart quality of dried cranberries is underlined by the distinctive bite of horseradish and the fresh flavor of scallions. And if you're wondering what the difference is between green onions and scallions, consider this: grocery stores label long, skinny, green-topped onions with white bottoms as either scallions or green onions, but they are almost always the exact same plant.

Tip: Wasabi (Japanese horseradish) may be used in place of traditional horseradish in this recipe. Use either 1 tbsp (15 mL) prepared wasabi paste or 2 tsp (10 mL) wasabi powder.

- Preheat oven to 400°F (200°C)
- 12-cup muffin pan, greased

2 cups	all-purpose flour	500 mL
1 tbsp	baking powder	15 mL
1/4 tsp	salt	1 mL
1/4 tsp	freshly ground black pepper	1 mL
1/3 cup	olive oil	75 mL
1 tbsp	prepared horseradish	15 mL
1 1/3 cups	non-dairy milk (soy, almond, rice, hemp)	325 mL
2/3 cup	chopped green onions (scallions)	150 mL
1/2 cup	dried cranberries, chopped	125 mL

1. In a large bowl, whisk together flour, baking powder, salt and pepper.

2. In a medium bowl, whisk together oil and horseradish until well blended. Whisk in milk until blended.

3. Add the milk mixture to the flour mixture and stir until just blended. Gently fold in green onions and cranberries.

4. Divide batter equally among prepared muffin cups.

5. Bake in preheated oven for 16 to 20 minutes or until tops are golden and a toothpick inserted in the center comes out clean. Let cool in pan on a wire rack for 5 minutes, then transfer to the rack. Serve warm or let cool completely.

Vidalia Onion Muffins

Makes 12 muffins

The Vidalia onion — the official vegetable of Georgia since 1990 — is renowned for its sweet, mild flavor. Although other sweet onions would make a fine substitute, Vidalia's signature sweetness is particularly gorgeous with the aromatic nuances of rosemary and the toasted nuttiness of pecans in these muffins. Serve with a salad and you've got a perfect summertime supper.

> **Tip:** Always use a sharp knife to slice or chop onions. A food processor or dull knife will rupture more of the onion's delicate cell structure, causing the release of more of its sulfur-containing amino acids. These come into contact with other enzymes in the onion, creating the sulfuric acid that makes you cry and makes the onion taste strong.

- Preheat oven to 400°F (200°C)
- 12-cup muffin pan, greased

1 cup	all-purpose flour	250 mL
1 cup	quick-cooking rolled oats	250 mL
1 1/2 tsp	baking powder	7 mL
1/2 tsp	salt	2 mL
1 tbsp	vegan granulated sugar or evaporated cane juice	15 mL
2 tsp	chopped fresh rosemary	10 mL
1 cup	non-dairy milk (soy, almond, rice, hemp)	250 mL
1/4 cup	olive oil	60 mL
3/4 cup	finely chopped Vidalia onion	175 mL
1/2 cup	chopped pecans, toasted	125 mL

1. In a large bowl, whisk together flour, oats, baking powder and salt.

2. In a medium bowl, whisk together sugar, rosemary, milk and oil until well blended. Stir in onion and pecans.

3. Add the milk mixture to the flour mixture and stir until just blended.

4. Divide batter equally among prepared muffin cups.

5. Bake in preheated oven for 16 to 20 minutes or until tops are golden and a toothpick inserted in the center comes out clean. Let cool in pan on a wire rack for 5 minutes, then transfer to the rack to cool.

Bell Pepper Basil Muffins

Makes 12 muffins

So often bell peppers play a supporting role to other ingredients; here, they take center stage, and fresh basil becomes the supporting player. The reviews are in: brilliant.

Tips: One 12-oz (375 mL) jar of roasted red bell peppers, drained and chopped, may be used in place of the fresh red bell peppers; skip step 1, omitting 1 tbsp (15 mL) of the oil, and simply combine the roasted peppers with the basil.

If you don't have fresh basil on hand, you can use 1 tbsp (15 mL) dried instead.

- 12-cup muffin pan, greased

6 tbsp	olive oil, divided	90 mL
2	red bell peppers, chopped	2
1/2 cup	fresh basil leaves, chopped	125 mL
1 1/2 cups	all-purpose flour	375 mL
1/2 cup	yellow cornmeal	125 mL
2 tsp	baking powder	10 mL
1 tsp	salt	5 mL
1/2 tsp	baking soda	2 mL
1 tbsp	vegan granulated sugar or evaporated cane juice	15 mL
1 1/4 cups	plain soy yogurt	300 mL

1. In a large skillet, heat 1 tbsp (15 mL) of the oil over medium-high heat. Add red peppers and cook, stirring, for 4 to 5 minutes or until softened. Remove from heat and stir in basil. Let cool.

2. Preheat oven to 425°F (220°C).

3. In a large bowl, whisk together flour, cornmeal, baking powder, salt and baking soda.

4. In a medium bowl, whisk together sugar, yogurt and the remaining oil until well blended.

5. Add the yogurt mixture to the flour mixture and stir until just blended. Gently fold in red pepper mixture.

6. Divide batter equally among prepared muffin cups.

7. Bake for 14 to 18 minutes or until a toothpick inserted in the center comes out clean. Let cool in pan on a wire rack for 3 minutes, then transfer to the rack to cool.

Chipotle Red Pepper Muffins

Makes 12 muffins

When mixed up with smoky spices and sweet roasted peppers, savory muffins become a delicious crowd-pleaser. There's enough chipotle here to make your lips just barely hum, but not so much as to overshadow the balancing act created by the other ingredients — garlic, cumin and a kiss of brown sugar.

- Preheat oven to 375°F (190°C)
- 12-cup muffin pan, greased

1½ cups	all-purpose flour	375 mL
½ cup	yellow cornmeal	125 mL
2½ tsp	baking powder	12 mL
1 tsp	chipotle pepper powder	5 mL
1 tsp	ground cumin	5 mL
½ tsp	garlic powder	2 mL
½ tsp	baking soda	2 mL
½ tsp	salt	2 mL
2 tbsp	light brown sugar	30 mL
¾ cup	plain soy yogurt	175 mL
½ cup	vegetable oil	125 mL
¾ cup	chopped drained roasted red bell peppers, patted dry	175 mL

1. In a large bowl, whisk together flour, cornmeal, baking powder, chipotle powder, cumin, garlic powder, baking soda and salt.

2. In a medium bowl, whisk together brown sugar, yogurt and oil until well blended. Stir in roasted peppers.

3. Add the yogurt mixture to the flour mixture and stir until just blended.

4. Divide batter equally among prepared muffin cups.

5. Bake in preheated oven for 18 to 22 minutes or until a toothpick inserted in the center comes out clean. Let cool in pan on a wire rack for 3 minutes, then transfer to the rack. Serve warm or let cool.

Muhammara Muffins

Makes 12 muffins

Muhammara (pronounced moo-HAHM-mer-ah) is a roasted red pepper purée seasoned with walnuts, pomegranate molasses and hot red pepper. Syria is the birthplace of muhammara, but it can be found in southern Turkey as well. I've captured the same multiplex of flavors in my muffin — a little sweet, a little savory, a little spicy — plus plenty of gorgeous red color from the roasted peppers.

- Preheat oven to 350°F (180°C)
- 12-cup muffin pan, lined with paper liners

2 cups	all-purpose flour	500 mL
1 tbsp	baking powder	15 mL
2 tsp	ground cumin	10 mL
1/2 tsp	salt	2 mL
1/4 tsp	cayenne pepper	1 mL
1/4 tsp	baking soda	1 mL
1 cup	walnut halves, toasted, finely chopped	250 mL
1 cup	non-dairy milk (soy, almond, rice, hemp)	250 mL
1/4 cup	olive oil	60 mL
1 tsp	finely grated lemon zest	5 mL
1 tbsp	freshly squeezed lemon juice	15 mL
1 tbsp	brown rice syrup or agave nectar	15 mL
1	jar (7 oz/210 mL) roasted red peppers, drained, patted dry and chopped	1

1. In a large bowl, whisk together flour, baking powder, cumin, salt, cayenne and baking soda. Stir in walnuts.

2. In a medium bowl, whisk together milk, oil, lemon zest, lemon juice and brown rice syrup until well blended.

3. Add the milk mixture to the flour mixture and stir until just blended. Gently fold in roasted peppers.

4. Divide batter equally among prepared muffin cups.

5. Bake in preheated oven for 21 to 25 minutes or until a toothpick inserted in the center comes out clean. Let cool in pan on a wire rack for 5 minutes, then transfer to the rack to cool.

Cherry Tomato Muffins

Makes 12 muffins

Delivering a lot of summer glamour for very little work, these gorgeous muffins find a perfect balance of tender, basil-flecked bread and sweet, fresh cherry tomatoes.

> **Tip:** Keep cherry tomatoes and all other tomatoes out of the refrigerator. Chilling destroys a key flavor component in tomatoes and makes the texture mealy. Ideally, tomatoes should be stored away from light, at about 50°F (10°C).

- Preheat oven to 400°F (200°C)
- 12-cup muffin pan, greased

2 cups	all-purpose flour	500 mL
2 tsp	baking powder	10 mL
1½ tsp	dried basil	7 mL
1 tsp	baking soda	5 mL
½ tsp	salt	2 mL
¼ tsp	freshly ground black pepper	1 mL
1 tbsp	vegan granulated sugar or evaporated cane juice	15 mL
¾ cup	plain non-dairy milk (soy, almond, rice, hemp)	175 mL
¾ cup	plain soy yogurt	175 mL
⅓ cup	olive oil	75 mL
1 cup	cherry tomatoes, quartered	250 mL

1. In a large bowl, whisk together flour, baking powder, basil, baking soda, salt and pepper.

2. In a medium bowl, whisk together sugar, milk, yogurt and oil until well blended.

3. Add the yogurt mixture to the flour mixture and stir until just blended. Gently fold in tomatoes.

4. Divide batter equally among prepared muffin cups.

5. Bake in preheated oven for 18 to 22 minutes or until tops are golden brown and a toothpick inserted in the center comes out clean. Let cool in pan on a wire rack for 3 minutes, then transfer to the rack. Serve warm or let cool.

Ancho Chile and Cherry Tomato Muffins

Makes 12 muffins

The slightly smoky hit of heat from ancho chile powder is a great foil for the bright, fresh flavor of tomatoes and the intense onion flavor of fresh green onions. Tomatoes of all varieties are high in vitamin C and lycopene. Green onions also have high levels of vitamin C, as well as vitamin A.

- Preheat oven to 400°F (200°C)
- 12-cup muffin pan, greased

1⅓ cups	non-dairy milk (soy, almond, rice, hemp)	325 mL
1 tbsp	cider vinegar	15 mL
2 cups	all-purpose flour	250 mL
½ cup	yellow cornmeal	125 mL
1 tbsp	baking powder	15 mL
1 tsp	ancho chile powder	5 mL
¾ tsp	ground cumin	3 mL
½ tsp	baking soda	2 mL
½ tsp	salt	2 mL
⅓ cup	vegetable oil	75 mL
1½ cups	cherry tomatoes, quartered	375 mL
½ cup	chopped green onions (scallions)	125 mL

1. In a glass measuring cup, combine milk and vinegar. Let stand for 5 minutes.

2. In a large bowl, whisk together flour, cornmeal, baking powder, ancho chile powder, cumin, baking soda and salt.

3. Whisk oil into the milk mixture until well blended. Add the milk mixture to the flour mixture and stir until just blended. Gently fold in tomatoes and green onions.

4. Divide batter equally among prepared muffin cups.

5. Bake in preheated oven for 20 to 25 minutes or until tops are light golden brown and a toothpick inserted in the center comes out clean. Let cool in pan on a wire rack for 3 minutes, then transfer to the rack to cool slightly. Serve warm.

Salsa Muffins

Makes 12 muffins

Salsa is great with chips, but it is also a fantastic pantry staple. Think about it: tomatoes, peppers, onions, spice and heat — it's a quick foundation for chili, soup, omelets and casseroles. I love what it does to a basic corn muffin, too. I especially like these when they're made with chipotle salsa, but any thick tomato salsa will do.

Tips: You can sprinkle the muffins with a bit of shredded vegan cheese alternative, such as Cheddar-style or Jack-style, before baking.

Serve these muffins with steaming bowls of vegan chili for a perfect mid-winter feast.

- Preheat oven to 400°F (200°C)
- 12-cup muffin pan, greased

1 cup	all-purpose flour	250 mL
1 cup	yellow cornmeal	250 mL
1 tbsp	baking powder	15 mL
1 tsp	ground cumin	5 mL
½ tsp	salt	2 mL
2 tsp	vegan granulated sugar or evaporated cane juice	10 mL
⅔ cup	non-dairy milk (soy, almond, rice, hemp)	150 mL
¼ cup	vegetable oil	60 mL
1 cup	bottled chunky tomato salsa	250 mL

1. In a large bowl, whisk together flour, cornmeal, baking powder, cumin and salt.

2. In a medium bowl, whisk together sugar, milk and oil until well blended. Stir in salsa until blended.

3. Add the salsa mixture to the flour mixture and stir until just blended.

4. Divide batter equally among prepared muffin cups.

5. Bake in preheated oven for 23 to 28 minutes or until tops are golden and a toothpick inserted in the center comes out clean. Let cool in pan on a wire rack for 5 minutes, then transfer to the rack. Serve warm or let cool completely.

Mediterranean Muffins

Makes 12 muffins

The labor in this recipe is minimal, and it pays tenfold (or more). The delectable (but healthy) result is great paired with soup, but one muffin is practically a meal unto itself.

- Preheat oven to 350°F (180°C)
- Blender
- 12-cup muffin pan, greased

1½ cups	all-purpose flour	375 mL
¾ cup	whole wheat flour	175 mL
2½ tsp	baking powder	12 mL
¾ tsp	dried basil	3 mL
¾ tsp	dried oregano	3 mL
½ tsp	salt	2 mL
3 tbsp	ground flax seeds	45 mL
1 cup	plain non-dairy milk (soy, almond, rice, hemp)	250 mL
¼ cup	olive oil	60 mL
⅓ cup	chopped walnuts, toasted	75 mL
⅓ cup	chopped pitted kalamata olives	75 mL
⅓ cup	chopped drained oil-packed sun-dried tomatoes	75 mL

1. In a medium bowl, whisk together all-purpose flour, whole wheat flour, baking powder, basil, oregano and salt.

2. In blender, process flax seeds and ½ cup (125 mL) water for 1 minute or until thickened and frothy. Add milk and oil; process for 2 minutes or until well blended and frothy.

3. Add the flax seed mixture to the flour mixture and stir until just blended. Gently fold in walnuts, olives and tomatoes.

4. Divide batter equally among prepared muffin cups.

5. Bake in preheated oven for 20 to 25 minutes or until tops are golden brown and a toothpick inserted in the center comes out clean. Let cool in pan on a wire rack for 5 minutes, then transfer to the rack. Serve warm or let cool.

Sun-Dried Tomato and Spinach Muffins

Makes 16 muffins

I love the umami flavor of sun-dried tomatoes; they impart a concentrated tomato flavor to everything they are added to. In addition, sun-dried tomatoes are a natural source of vitamin C and iron.

Tip: Frozen spinach can have a higher nutrient profile than fresh. Fresh spinach quickly loses much of its nutritional value when it is exposed to air and light. But when spinach is flash-frozen almost immediately after picking, its nutrients are preserved.

- Preheat oven to 375°F (190°C)
- Two 12-cup muffin pans, 16 cups greased

2 cups	whole wheat pastry flour	500 mL
1 cup	all-purpose flour	250 mL
2½ tsp	baking powder	12 mL
1 tsp	dried basil	5 mL
½ tsp	salt	2 mL
1 tbsp	vegan granulated sugar or evaporated cane juice	15 mL
⅓ cup	olive oil	60 mL
1⅓ cups	non-dairy milk (soy, almond, rice, hemp)	325 mL
1	package (10 oz/300 g) frozen chopped spinach, thawed and squeezed dry	1
⅓ cup	chopped drained oil-packed sun-dried tomatoes	75 mL

1. In a large bowl, whisk together whole wheat pastry flour, all-purpose flour, baking powder, basil and salt.

2. In a medium bowl, whisk together sugar and oil until well blended. Whisk in milk until blended. Stir in spinach and tomatoes.

3. Add the milk mixture to the flour mixture and stir until just blended.

4. Divide batter equally among prepared muffin cups.

5. Bake in preheated oven for 18 to 23 minutes or until a toothpick inserted in the center comes out clean. Let cool in pans on a wire rack for 3 minutes, then transfer to the rack to cool.

Mashed Potato Muffins

Makes 12 muffins

I am not dismissing the appeal of mashed potatoes as is, but tender, crusty muffins made from the leftovers are simply terrific. Here, I've kept the embellishments simple: a sprinkling of black pepper and green onions.

> **Tip:** For the best texture in these muffins, mash the potatoes with a fork; do not purée.

- Preheat oven to 400°F (200°C)
- 12-cup muffin pan, greased

1 cup	all-purpose flour	250 mL
1/3 cup	yellow cornmeal	75 mL
1 tbsp	baking powder	15 mL
3/4 tsp	salt	3 mL
1/4 tsp	freshly ground black pepper	1 mL
1 tbsp	vegan granulated sugar or evaporated cane juice	15 mL
1 1/3 cups	prepared vegan mashed potatoes, at room temperature	325 mL
1/4 cup	vegan margarine, melted	60 mL
1 cup	non-dairy milk (soy, almond, rice, hemp)	250 mL
1/2 cup	finely chopped green onions (scallions)	125 mL

1. In a large bowl, whisk together flour, cornmeal, baking powder, salt and pepper.

2. In a medium bowl, whisk together sugar, mashed potatoes and margarine until well blended. Whisk in milk until blended. Stir in green onions.

3. Add the potato mixture to the flour mixture and stir until just blended.

4. Divide batter equally among prepared muffin cups.

5. Bake in preheated oven for 15 to 19 minutes or until tops are golden and a toothpick inserted in the center comes out clean. Let cool in pan on a wire rack for 5 minutes, then transfer to the rack. Serve warm or let cool completely.

Sweet Potato Sage Muffins

Makes 12 muffins

Sweet potatoes take beautifully to muffin form. The sage and green onions make an ideal foil for the sweetness of the potatoes.

> **Tips:** Be careful measuring the sage for this recipe. Although the musky, minty and slightly floral flavor of the herb is delectable in combination with the sweet potatoes, it is very pungent: too much and the flavor can be overwhelming.
>
> If making the mashed sweet potatoes from scratch, prepare them without milk and butter. They can be easily prepared in the microwave: Scrub sweet potatoes (about 2 medium for this recipe) and pierce each a few times with a fork. Place on a microwave-safe plate lined with a paper towel. Microwave on High, turning halfway through, for 4 to 5 minutes for the first potato plus 2 to 3 minutes for each additional potato. Let cool. Cut in half, scoop the flesh into a bowl and mash with a fork.

- Preheat oven to 350°F (180°C)
- 12-cup muffin pan, greased

¾ cup	non-dairy milk (soy, almond, rice, hemp)	175 mL
2 tsp	cider vinegar	10 mL
2¼ cups	all-purpose flour	550 mL
2½ tsp	baking powder	12 mL
1½ tsp	salt	7 mL
1 tsp	dried sage	5 mL
½ tsp	baking soda	2 mL
2 tbsp	vegan granulated sugar or evaporated cane juice	30 mL
⅓ cup	vegetable oil	75 mL
1	can (15 oz/425 mL) sweet potatoes, drained and mashed (or 1½ cups/ 375 mL cold mashed cooked sweet potatoes)	1
⅓ cup	finely chopped green onions (scallions)	75 mL

1. In a glass measuring cup, combine milk and vinegar. Let stand for 5 minutes.

2. In a large bowl, whisk together flour, baking powder, salt, sage and baking soda.

3. In a medium bowl, whisk together sugar, milk mixture and oil until well blended. Stir in sweet potatoes until blended.

4. Add the sweet potato mixture to the flour mixture and stir until just blended. Gently fold in green onions.

5. Divide batter equally among prepared muffin cups.

6. Bake in preheated oven for 22 to 27 minutes or until tops are golden and a toothpick inserted in the center comes out clean. Let cool in pan on a wire rack for 5 minutes, then transfer to the rack. Serve warm or let cool completely.

Zucchini Cornbread Muffins

Makes 12 muffins

A generous helping of fresh zucchini gives cornbread muffins seasonal flair.

> **Tips:** While small to medium zucchini are ideal for sautéing, grilling or eating raw, the jumbo ones (think doorstop-size) are great in baked goods. If you have a particularly large zucchini bounty, you can shred it and freeze it for several months.
>
> Look for shiny, dark green zucchini (the freshest ones will have slightly prickly skin). They should be firm to the touch and heavy in your hand. Avoid zucchini with breaks, gashes or soft spots. Store zucchini in the refrigerator for 1 to 2 weeks.

- Preheat oven to 400°F (200°C)
- 12-cup muffin pan, greased

2 cups	non-dairy milk (soy, almond, rice, hemp)	500 mL
1 1/2 tbsp	cider vinegar	22 mL
1 1/4 cups	yellow cornmeal	300 mL
1 1/4 cups	all-purpose flour	300 mL
2 1/2 tsp	baking powder	12 mL
1 tsp	salt	5 mL
1 tsp	ground cumin	5 mL
1/2 tsp	baking soda	2 mL
1/8 tsp	cayenne pepper	0.5 mL
1 tbsp	vegan granulated sugar or evaporated cane juice	45 mL
1/4 cup	vegetable oil	60 mL
1 cup	shredded zucchini	250 mL

1. In a glass measuring cup, combine milk and vinegar. Let stand for 5 minutes.

2. In a large bowl, whisk together cornmeal, flour, baking powder, salt, cumin, baking soda and cayenne.

3. In a medium bowl, whisk together sugar and oil until well blended. Whisk in milk mixture until blended. Stir in zucchini.

4. Add the zucchini mixture to the flour mixture and stir until just blended.

5. Divide batter equally among prepared muffin cups.

6. Bake in preheated oven for 23 to 26 minutes or until tops are golden and a toothpick inserted in the center comes out clean. Let cool in pan on a wire rack for 3 minutes, then transfer to the rack to cool. Serve warm or let cool.

Wild Rice Hazelnut Muffins

Makes 12 muffins

These hearty, nutty muffins are very easy to prepare, but the addition of cooked wild rice adds an unusual and marvelous twist to the simple batter. They are decidedly cold-weather fare; make a fresh batch to accompany a big batch of black bean chili or vegetable stew.

> **Tip:** You can also use your microwave to cook the wild rice: Combine the wild rice with 2¼ cups (550 mL) water in an 8-cup (2 L) microwave-safe container. Cover and microwave on High for 5 minutes. Microwave on Medium (50%) for 30 minutes. Let stand for 15 minutes, then drain and let cool.

- 12-cup muffin pan, greased

¾ cup	wild rice	175 mL
1 cup	all-purpose flour	250 mL
1½ tsp	baking powder	7 mL
1 tsp	salt	5 mL
3 tbsp	ground flax seeds	45 mL
2 tbsp	vegan granulated sugar or evaporated cane juice	30 mL
⅓ cup	olive oil or vegetable oil	75 mL
1¼ cups	finely chopped onion	300 mL
½ cup	chopped hazelnuts, toasted	125 mL

1. In a saucepan, combine wild rice and enough water to cover rice by 1 inch (2.5 cm). Bring to a boil over high heat. Reduce heat to medium-low, cover and simmer for about 45 minutes or until tender. Drain and let cool.

2. Preheat oven to 425°F (220°C).

3. In a large bowl, whisk together flour, baking powder and salt.

4. In blender, process flax seeds and ⅓ cup (75 mL) water for 1 minute or until thickened and frothy. Add sugar and oil; process until well blended.

5. Add the flax mixture to the flour mixture and stir until just blended. Stir in rice, onion and hazelnuts.

6. Divide batter equally among prepared muffin cups.

7. Bake for 19 to 22 minutes or until tops are golden and a toothpick inserted in the center comes out clean. Let cool in pan on a wire rack for 5 minutes, then transfer to the rack. Serve warm or let cool completely.

Spiced Pistachio Muffins

Makes 12 muffins

Pistachios make for an unusual but addictive muffin. Try making them in miniature muffin pans for the perfect cocktail snack.

Tip: When you purchase a spice, write the date on the container so you can easily gauge its freshness. After 6 months to a year, most spices have lost so much potency that they should be replaced.

- Preheat oven to 375°F (190°C)
- 12-cup muffin pan, greased

2 cups	all-purpose flour	500 mL
1 tbsp	baking powder	15 mL
2 tsp	mild curry powder	10 mL
1 tsp	ground coriander	5 mL
1/2 tsp	salt	2 mL
1/2 tsp	ground ginger	2 mL
1/2 tsp	ground cumin	2 mL
1/4 tsp	cayenne pepper	1 mL
1/8 tsp	ground cinnamon	0.5 mL
1 1/4 cups	non-dairy milk (soy, almond, rice, hemp)	300 mL
1/4 cup	olive oil	60 mL
3/4 cup	salted roasted pistachios, coarsely chopped	175 mL

1. In a large bowl, whisk together flour, baking powder, curry powder, coriander, salt, ginger, cumin, cayenne and cinnamon.

2. In a medium bowl, whisk together milk and oil until well blended.

3. Add the milk mixture to the flour mixture and stir until just blended. Gently fold in pistachios.

4. Divide batter equally among prepared muffin cups.

5. Bake in preheated oven for 18 to 22 minutes or until tops are golden and a toothpick inserted in the center comes out clean. Let cool in pan on a wire rack for 5 minutes, then transfer to the rack. Serve warm or let cool completely.

Toasted Walnut Muffins

Makes 12 muffins

Toasted walnuts are rich and flavorful unadorned, but they get added personality when stirred into a faintly sweet whole wheat batter.

> **Tip:** Toasting intensifies the flavor of nuts, but pay attention as you toast. Nuts are delicate — they can go from perfectly toasty to charred in seconds. Nuts are done toasting when they've darkened slightly (or turned golden brown for pale nuts such as pine nuts or slivered almonds) and smell fragrant and toasty.

- Preheat oven to 375°F (190°C)
- 12-cup muffin pan, lined with paper liners

1 cup	all-purpose flour	250 mL
1 cup	whole wheat flour	250 mL
2 tsp	baking powder	10 mL
½ tsp	salt	2 mL
½ tsp	baking soda	2 mL
2 tbsp	packed vegan light brown sugar or Sucanat	30 mL
¾ cup	non-dairy milk (soy, almond, rice, hemp)	175 mL
¾ cup	plain soy yogurt	175 mL
½ cup	walnut oil or olive oil	125 mL
1⅓ cups	chopped walnuts, toasted	325 mL

1. In a large bowl, whisk together all-purpose flour, whole wheat flour, baking powder, salt and baking soda.

2. In a medium bowl, whisk together brown sugar, milk, yogurt and oil until well blended.

3. Add the yogurt mixture to the flour mixture and stir until just blended. Gently fold in walnuts.

4. Divide batter equally among prepared muffin cups.

5. Bake in preheated oven for 20 to 25 minutes or until tops are golden and a toothpick inserted in the center comes out clean. Let cool in pan on a wire rack for 5 minutes, then transfer to the rack. Serve warm or let cool completely.

Caraway Muffins

Makes 12 muffins

Crushing the caraway seeds greatly enhances their aromatic flavor. The process is a snap: place the seeds in a small sealable plastic bag, seal and pound the seeds with a mallet or rolling pin until they're coarsely crushed.

> **Tip:** Caraway, native to northern Africa, the Mediterranean and much of Europe, has a spectacular history in addition to its distinctive, anise-like flavor. Caraway seeds have been found in food dating back to 3000 BC, making it one of the oldest cultivated spices. The ancient Egyptians buried their dead with caraway to ward off evil spirits. It was used in both foods and medicines in ancient Greece and Rome, and it was used as a love potion in northern Africa.

- Preheat oven to 375°F (190°C)
- 12-cup muffin pan, greased

1¼ cups	non-dairy milk (soy, almond, rice, hemp)	300 mL
1 tbsp	cider vinegar	15 mL
1⅓ cups	all-purpose flour	325 mL
⅔ cup	whole wheat flour	150 mL
1 tbsp	caraway seeds, crushed	15 mL
2 tsp	baking powder	10 mL
1 tsp	salt	5 mL
½ tsp	baking soda	2 mL
¼ cup	vegan margarine, melted	60 mL
3 tbsp	packed vegan light brown sugar or Sucanat	45 mL
1 tsp	finely grated orange zest	5 mL

1. In a glass measuring cup, combine milk and vinegar. Let stand for 5 minutes.

2. In a large bowl, whisk together all-purpose flour, whole wheat flour, caraway seeds, baking powder, salt and baking soda.

3. In a medium bowl, whisk together margarine, brown sugar and orange zest until well blended. Whisk in milk mixture until blended.

4. Add the milk mixture to the flour mixture and stir until just blended.

5. Divide batter equally among prepared muffin cups.

6. Bake in preheated oven for 22 to 26 minutes or until tops are golden and a toothpick inserted in the center comes out clean. Let cool in pan on a wire rack for 3 minutes, then transfer to the rack. Serve warm or let cool completely.

Seeded Bulgur Muffins

Makes 18 muffins

Who knew that cracked wheat (also known as bulgur) could be so delicious? Okay, I knew; I think bulgur is scrumptious in almost any form. You will be convinced of its excellence too once you sample these muffins. They have great substance and fantastic flavor, with a satisfying mix of seeds throughout.

> **Tips:** You can use any type of cracked wheat, from fine to coarse grinds, for this recipe — they all work well.
>
> For an even healthier muffin, replace half of the all-purpose flour with whole wheat flour.

● Two 12-cup muffin pans, 18 cups greased

½ cup	cracked wheat (bulgur)	125 mL
½ cup	boiling water	125 mL
3 cups	all-purpose flour	750 mL
1½ tbsp	baking powder	22 mL
¾ tsp	salt	3 mL
1 tbsp	packed vegan light brown sugar or Sucanat	15 mL
3	jars (each 4 oz or 128 mL) squash or carrot purée baby food	3
¾ cup	non-dairy milk (soy, almond, rice, hemp)	175 mL
½ cup	olive oil or vegetable oil	125 mL
2 tbsp	poppy seeds	30 mL
2 tbsp	sesame seeds	30 mL

1. In a small bowl, combine cracked wheat and boiling water. Let stand, uncovered, for about 30 minutes or until water is absorbed.

2. Preheat oven to 400°F (200°C).

3. In a large bowl, whisk together flour, baking powder and salt.

4. In a medium bowl, whisk together brown sugar, squash, milk, oil and poppy seeds until well blended. Stir in cracked wheat.

5. Add the squash mixture to the flour mixture and stir until just blended.

6. Sprinkle sesame seeds in the bottoms of prepared muffin cups and gently shake so some stick to the sides. Divide batter equally among cups.

7. Bake for 23 to 28 minutes or until tops are golden brown and a toothpick inserted in the center comes out clean. Let cool in pans on a wire rack for 5 minutes, then transfer to the rack. Serve warm or let cool completely.

Three-Seed Muffins

Makes 12 muffins

Poppy, caraway and sesame seeds provide just the right amount of flavor and texture in these slightly sweet, down-home muffins.

- Preheat oven to 400°F (200°C)
- 12-cup muffin pan, greased

1 1/2 cups	all-purpose flour	375 mL
1/2 cup	whole wheat flour	125 mL
2 tbsp	sesame seeds, divided	30 mL
1 tbsp	baking powder	15 mL
1 tbsp	poppy seeds	15 mL
1 tbsp	caraway seeds	15 mL
1 tsp	salt	5 mL
2 tbsp	packed vegan dark brown sugar or Sucanat	30 mL
1/3 cup	olive oil	75 mL
1 1/3 cups	non-dairy milk (soy, almond, rice, hemp)	325 mL

1. In a large bowl, whisk together all-purpose flour, whole wheat flour, 1 tbsp (15 mL) of the sesame seeds, baking powder, poppy seeds, caraway seeds and salt.

2. In a medium bowl, whisk together brown sugar and oil until well blended. Whisk in milk until blended.

3. Add the milk mixture to the flour mixture and stir until just blended.

4. Divide batter equally among prepared muffin cups. Sprinkle with the remaining sesame seeds.

5. Bake in preheated oven for 18 to 22 minutes or until tops are golden and a toothpick inserted in the center comes out clean. Let cool in pan on a wire rack for 5 minutes, then transfer to the rack. Serve warm or let cool completely.

Chickpea Muffins with Indian Spices

Makes 10 muffins

Chickpea flour adds nutty flavor to this quick and savory supper bread. Pumpkin keeps the muffins moist, and a panoply of Indian spices makes them exciting.

- Preheat oven to 350°F (180°C)
- 12-cup muffin pan, 10 cups greased

1 1/2 cups	whole wheat pastry flour	375 mL
1/2 cup	chickpea flour	125 mL
2 tsp	ground cumin	10 mL
2 tsp	garam masala	10 mL
1 tsp	baking powder	5 mL
1 tsp	salt	5 mL
1/2 tsp	baking soda	2 mL
1/8 tsp	cayenne pepper	0.5 mL
1/4 cup	pumpkin purée (not pie filling)	60 mL
2 tbsp	toasted sesame oil	30 mL
2 tbsp	agave nectar	30 mL
1 1/4 cups	plain non-dairy milk (soy, almond, rice, hemp)	300 mL

1. In a large bowl, whisk together whole wheat pastry flour, chickpea flour, cumin, garam masala, baking powder, salt, baking soda and cayenne.

2. In a medium bowl, whisk together pumpkin, oil and agave nectar until well blended. Whisk in milk until blended.

3. Add the pumpkin mixture to the flour mixture and stir until just blended.

4. Divide batter equally among prepared muffin cups.

5. Bake in preheated oven for 18 to 22 minutes or until tops are golden brown and a toothpick inserted in the center comes out clean. Let cool in pan on a wire rack for 5 minutes, then transfer to the rack. Serve warm or let cool.

Madras Curry Muffins

These muffins feature the flavors of India: aromatic curry powder, yogurt and cumin. I love to pair them with chopped vegetable salads or chilled soup on steamy Texas summer nights.

- Preheat oven to 375°F (190°C)
- 12-cup muffin pan, lined with paper liners

2½ cups	all-purpose flour	625 mL
1 tbsp	mild curry powder	15 mL
2½ tsp	baking powder	12 mL
1 tsp	ground cumin	5 mL
1 tsp	baking soda	5 mL
1 tsp	salt	5 mL
1 tbsp	vegan granulated sugar or evaporated cane juice	15 mL
1 cup	plain soy yogurt	250 mL
½ cup	non-dairy milk (soy, almond, rice, hemp)	125 mL
⅓ cup	vegetable oil	75 mL
¾ cup	chopped green onions (scallions)	175 mL
⅓ cup	golden raisins, chopped	75 mL

1. In a large bowl, whisk together flour, curry powder, baking powder, cumin, baking soda and salt.

2. In a medium bowl, whisk together sugar, yogurt, milk and oil until well blended.

3. Add the yogurt mixture to the flour mixture and stir until just blended. Gently fold in green onions and raisins.

4. Divide batter equally among prepared muffin cups.

5. Bake in preheated oven for 22 to 27 minutes or until tops are golden and a toothpick inserted in the center comes out clean. Let cool in pan on a wire rack for 3 minutes, then transfer to the rack. Serve warm or let cool completely.

Beer Batter Muffins

Makes 12 muffins

For a different take on dinner rolls, a few pantry staples are spiked with beer and fortified by vegan margarine. The beer contributes a maltiness to the muffins that pairs well with a wide range of soups and suppers.

- Preheat oven to 375°F (190°C)
- 12-cup muffin pan, greased

3 cups	all-purpose flour	750 mL
3 tbsp	vegan granulated sugar or evaporated cane juice	45 mL
1 tbsp	baking powder	15 mL
1 tsp	salt	5 mL
1	bottle (12 oz/341 mL) beer, at room temperature	1
1/4 cup	vegan margarine, melted	60 mL

1. In a large bowl, whisk together flour, sugar, baking powder and salt.

2. Add beer and margarine to the flour mixture all at once and stir as little as possible until just blended.

3. Divide batter equally among prepared muffin cups.

4. Bake in preheated oven for 22 to 25 minutes or until tops are golden and a toothpick inserted in the center comes out clean. Let cool in pan on a wire rack for 5 minutes, then transfer to the rack. Serve warm or let cool completely.

Guinness Muffins

Makes 12 muffins

The malt flavor of Guinness marries deliciously with the rye and brown sugar in these distinctive muffins, and the faintly bitter aftertaste cuts the sweetness.

Tip: Guinness and other Irish stouts produce a thick head when poured, so chill the can or bottle well to reduce the foam before adding the beer to the batter.

- Preheat oven to 350°F (180°C)
- 12-cup muffin pan, greased

2 cups	all-purpose flour	500 mL
1 cup	rye flour	250 mL
1 tsp	caraway seeds	5 mL
½ tsp	baking soda	2 mL
½ tsp	salt	2 mL
¼ cup	packed vegan dark brown sugar or Sucanat	60 mL
¼ cup	vegan margarine, melted	60 mL
1	bottle (12 oz/341 mL) Guinness or other dark beer	1

1. In a large bowl, whisk together all-purpose flour, rye flour, caraway seeds, baking soda and salt.

2. In a medium bowl, whisk together brown sugar and margarine until blended.

3. Add the brown sugar mixture and Guinness to the flour mixture and stir until just blended.

4. Divide batter equally among prepared muffin cups.

5. Bake in preheated oven for 24 to 28 minutes or until tops are golden and a toothpick inserted in the center comes out clean. Let cool in pan on a wire rack for 5 minutes, then transfer to the rack. Serve warm or let cool completely.

Global Muffins

Mexican Chocolate Muffins (Mexico)

Makes 12 muffins

I find it extremely challenging to stop at just one of these spicy chocolate muffins. They are so simple to prepare, too.

- Preheat oven to 350°F (180°C)
- Blender
- 12-cup muffin pan, greased

1¼ cups	all-purpose flour	300 mL
½ cup	unsweetened cocoa powder (not Dutch process)	125 mL
1 tsp	baking powder	15 mL
¾ tsp	ground cinnamon	3 mL
½ tsp	baking soda	2 mL
½ tsp	salt	2 mL
⅛ tsp	cayenne pepper	0.5 mL
½ cup	packed vegan dark brown sugar or Sucanat	125 mL
⅔ cup	soft silken tofu	150 mL
⅔ cup	plain soy yogurt	150 mL
⅓ cup	vegetable oil	75 mL
½ tsp	almond extract	2 mL
½ cup	vegan miniature semisweet chocolate chips	125 mL

1. In a large bowl, whisk together flour, cocoa powder, baking powder, cinnamon, baking soda, salt and cayenne.

2. In blender, process brown sugar, tofu, yogurt, oil and almond extract until blended and smooth.

3. Add the tofu mixture to the flour mixture and stir until just blended. Gently fold in chocolate chips.

4. Divide batter equally among prepared muffin cups.

5. Bake in preheated oven for 21 to 25 minutes or until tops are firm and a toothpick inserted in the center comes out clean. Let cool in pan on a wire rack for 3 minutes, then transfer to the rack to cool.

Rum and Coconut Muffins (Jamaica)

Makes 12 muffins

You could buy a ticket to the tropics, or you could simply make these muffins. Heady with rum and sweet flaked coconut, these incredibly easy, super-delicious muffins will transport you to a table in the sand, under the swaying palms. If only every recipe could be this straightforward and rewarding.

Tip: Coconut milk will last indefinitely in an unopened can or Tetra Pak, but it is as highly perishable as dairy milk once opened. Refrigerate the milk and use it within 3 days. It can also be frozen for up to 2 months.

- Preheat oven to 350°F (180°C)
- 12-cup muffin pan, greased

2 cups	all-purpose flour	500 mL
2 tsp	baking powder	10 mL
½ tsp	salt	2 mL
½ cup	packed vegan dark brown sugar or Sucanat	125 mL
¼ cup	vegetable oil, softened	60 mL
1¼ cups	coconut milk, well stirred	300 mL
2 tbsp	dark rum	30 mL
1 tsp	coconut flavoring	5 mL
1½ cups	sweetened flaked or shredded coconut, divided	375 mL

1. In a large bowl, whisk together flour, baking powder and salt.

2. In a medium bowl, whisk together brown sugar and oil until well blended. Whisk in coconut milk, rum and coconut flavoring until blended.

3. Add the coconut milk mixture to the flour mixture and stir until just blended. Gently fold in 1 cup (250 mL) of the coconut.

4. Divide batter equally among prepared muffin cups. Sprinkle with the remaining coconut.

5. Bake in preheated oven for 23 to 27 minutes or until tops are golden and a toothpick inserted in the center comes out clean. Let cool in pan on a wire rack for 5 minutes, then transfer to the rack to cool.

Raspberry Trifle Muffins (England)

Makes 12 muffins

Trifle is not only one of the most elegant desserts around, but also one of the most exuberant, which is why I had to recreate it as a muffin. These muffins have many of the hallmarks of traditional trifle, including a delicate crumb, dollops of raspberry jam, a hint of sherry and a creamy vanilla filling.

- Preheat oven to 400°F (200°C)
- 12-cup muffin pan, lined with paper liners

Filling

3 oz	non-dairy cream cheese (such as Tofutti brand), softened	90 g
2 tbsp	vegan confectioners' (icing) sugar	30 mL
1/2 tsp	vanilla extract	2 mL

Muffins

2 cups	all-purpose flour	500 mL
2 1/2 tsp	baking powder	12 mL
1/2 tsp	salt	2 mL
2/3 cup	vegan granulated sugar or evaporated cane juice	150 mL
1 cup	non-dairy milk (soy, almond, rice, hemp)	250 mL
1/2 cup	vegan margarine, melted	125 mL
2 tbsp	sherry	30 mL
1 1/2 cups	raspberries, divided	375 mL
1/4 cup	seedless raspberry jam	60 mL

1. *Filling:* In a small bowl, combine cream cheese, confectioners' sugar and vanilla until smooth.

2. *Muffins:* In a large bowl, whisk together flour, baking powder and salt.

3. In a medium bowl, whisk together sugar, milk, margarine and sherry until well blended.

4. Add the milk mixture to the flour mixture and stir until just blended. Gently stir in 3/4 cup (175 mL) of the raspberries.

5. Divide half the batter equally among prepared muffin cups. Spoon 1 tsp (5 mL) jam and 2 tsp (10 mL) filling into the center of each cup. Top with the remaining batter. Gently press the remaining berries into batter.

6. Bake in preheated oven for 19 to 23 minutes or until tops are golden and firm to the touch. Let cool in pan on a wire rack for 5 minutes, then transfer to the rack to cool.

Santa Lucia Muffins (Sweden)

Makes 12 muffins

Swedish lore has it that on December 13, 1764, a gentleman was awakened in the middle of the night by the singing of a young, winged woman in white. It was Saint Lucia and she arrived bearing light, food and wine as comfort on what was, in the Gregorian calendar, the longest night of the year. Saint Lucia continues to be celebrated on December 13 in Sweden, marked by children walking with lit candles, singing the beautiful Lucia carol and bringing Lucia bread. This yeast-free, muffin interpretation of Santa Lucia buns will give you a taste of the beauty and magic of the day.

Tip: Although the flavor will be quite different, you may use other spices in place of the saffron. For example, try $\frac{1}{4}$ tsp (1 mL) ground cloves or $\frac{1}{2}$ tsp (2 mL) ground cardamom. Do not soak the spices in boiling water; instead, whisk them into the flour mixture along with the baking powder and salt.

- Preheat oven to 375°F (190°C)
- 12-cup muffin pan, greased

1 tbsp	boiling water	15 mL
Pinch	saffron threads	Pinch
2 cups	all-purpose flour	500 mL
1 tbsp	baking powder	15 mL
$\frac{1}{2}$ tsp	salt	2 mL
$\frac{2}{3}$ cup	vegan granulated sugar or evaporated cane juice	150 mL
$\frac{1}{2}$ cup	vegan margarine, softened	125 mL
1 cup	non-dairy milk (soy, almond, rice, hemp)	250 mL
$\frac{1}{2}$ cup	dried currants or chopped raisins	125 mL

1. In a small bowl, combine boiling water and saffron. Let stand for 5 minutes.

2. In a medium bowl, whisk together flour, baking powder and salt.

3. In a large bowl, using an electric mixer on medium speed, beat sugar and margarine until light and fluffy. Beat in saffron mixture.

4. With the mixer on low speed, beat in flour mixture alternately with milk, making three additions of flour and two of milk, until just blended. Gently fold in currants.

5. Divide batter equally among prepared muffin cups.

6. Bake in preheated oven for 15 to 20 minutes or until a toothpick inserted in the center comes out clean. Let cool in pan on a wire rack for 5 minutes, then transfer to the rack to cool.

Dutch Spice Muffins (Holland)

Makes 12 muffins

Nothing irks me more than a spice muffin, cookie or cake that has but a hint of spice. Not so with these muffins. They are intensely spiced and very moist. And they only get better with age, so try to resist eating too many at once.

> **Tip:** An equal amount of whole wheat flour may be used in place of the rye flour.

- Preheat oven to 350°F (180°C)
- 12-cup muffin pan, greased

1½ cups	all-purpose flour	375 mL
½ cup	rye flour	125 mL
1 tbsp	baking powder	15 mL
1 tsp	salt	5 mL
1 tsp	ground cinnamon	5 mL
1 tsp	ground ginger	5 mL
½ tsp	ground nutmeg	2 mL
½ tsp	ground cardamom	2 mL
¼ tsp	ground cloves	1 mL
½ cup	packed vegan dark brown sugar or Sucanat	125 mL
1 cup	vanilla-flavored soy milk	250 mL
⅓ cup	dark (cooking) molasses	75 mL

1. In a large bowl, whisk together all-purpose flour, rye flour, baking powder, salt, cinnamon, ginger, nutmeg, cardamom and cloves.

2. In a medium bowl, whisk together brown sugar, milk and molasses until well blended.

3. Add the milk mixture to the flour mixture and stir until just blended.

4. Divide batter equally among prepared muffin cups.

5. Bake in preheated oven for 24 to 28 minutes or until a toothpick inserted in the center comes out clean. Let cool in pan on a wire rack for 5 minutes, then transfer to the rack to cool.

Green Olive Almond Muffins (Spain)

Makes 12 muffins

Olives and almonds are common offerings in many tapas restaurants across Spain. The combination also works wonders in these tender muffins.

Tip: Just a small handful of almonds contains as much calcium as $1/2$ cup (125 mL) of dairy milk, and 1 ounce (30 g) of almonds contains 2 g of fiber, the same as an apple or orange. Almonds also provide magnesium and potassium.

- Preheat oven to 375°F (190°C)
- 12-cup muffin pan, lined with paper liners

$1\frac{1}{4}$ cups	non-dairy milk (soy, almond, rice, hemp)	300 mL
$1\frac{1}{2}$ tbsp	sherry vinegar or cider vinegar	22 mL
2 cups	all-purpose flour	500 mL
2 tsp	baking powder	10 mL
1 tsp	dried oregano	5 mL
$\frac{1}{2}$ tsp	salt	5 mL
$\frac{1}{2}$ tsp	baking soda	5 mL
$\frac{1}{2}$ cup	olive oil	125 mL
$\frac{3}{4}$ cup	chopped pitted green olives	175 mL
$\frac{1}{2}$ cup	sliced almonds, toasted	125 mL

1. In a glass measuring cup, combine milk and vinegar. Let stand for 5 minutes.

2. In a large bowl, whisk together flour, baking powder, oregano, salt and baking soda.

3. Whisk oil into the milk mixture until well blended. Add the milk mixture to the flour mixture and stir until just blended. Gently fold in olives and almonds.

4. Divide batter equally among prepared muffin cups.

5. Bake in preheated oven for 20 to 25 minutes or until tops are golden and a toothpick inserted in the center comes out clean. Let cool in pan on a wire rack for 5 minutes, then transfer to the rack to cool.

Citrus Olive Oil Muffins (Spain)

Makes 16 muffins

My friends Anna and Jim spent a year living in Seville, and my husband and I were lucky enough to visit them during their stay. I'll never forget walking the orange-tree-lined streets, nor the scent of orange blossoms that perfumed the air. As an homage, I created this muffin. The refreshing flavor of orange, mingled with subtle olive oil, makes for a guaranteed favorite.

- Preheat oven to 375°F (190°C)
- Two 12-cup muffin pans, 16 cups greased

Muffins

¼ cup	finely grated orange zest (about 4 navel oranges)	60 mL
2 tbsp	freshly squeezed orange juice	30 mL
½ cup	vegan granulated sugar or evaporated cane juice, divided	125 mL
2 cups	all-purpose flour	500 mL
1½ tsp	baking powder	7 mL
1 tsp	baking soda	5 mL
½ tsp	salt	2 mL
⅓ cup	olive oil	75 mL
1½ cups	plain soy yogurt	375 mL

Glaze

1 cup	vegan confectioners' (icing) sugar	250 mL
1 tsp	finely grated orange zest	5 mL
2 tbsp	freshly squeezed orange juice	30 mL

1. *Muffins:* In a small saucepan, combine orange zest, orange juice and ¼ cup (60 mL) of the sugar. Bring to a simmer over medium heat. Simmer, stirring, for 2 to 3 minutes or until sugar is dissolved. Remove from heat and let cool slightly.

2. In a large bowl, whisk together flour, baking powder, baking soda and salt.

3. In a medium bowl, whisk together orange mixture, the remaining sugar and oil until well blended. Whisk in yogurt until blended.

4. Add the yogurt mixture to the flour mixture and stir until just blended.

5. Divide batter equally among prepared muffin cups.

6. Bake in preheated oven for 18 to 22 minutes or until tops are golden and a toothpick inserted in the center comes out clean. Let cool in pans on a wire rack for 5 minutes, then transfer to the rack to cool while you prepare the glaze.

7. *Glaze:* In a small bowl, whisk together confectioners' sugar, orange zest and orange juice until blended. Spoon over tops of warm muffins and let cool.

Pain d'Épices Muffins (France)

Makes 12 muffins

Pain d'épices is a dark, aromatic French loaf, part cake, part bread, with a mélange of spices and a hint of citrus. These gorgeous dark muffins taste just like the real thing; all you need is a cup of tea.

Tip: To easily crush the anise seeds, place them in a small, sealable plastic bag and seal it, pressing out as much air as possible. Place the bag on a cutting board and pound the seeds with a rolling pin or kitchen mallet.

- 12-cup muffin pan, greased

1 cup	non-dairy milk (soy, almond, rice, hemp)	250 mL
¾ cup	light molasses or brown rice syrup	175 mL
½ cup	packed vegan dark brown sugar or Sucanat	125 mL
2 cups	all-purpose flour	500 mL
½ cup	dark rye flour	125 mL
1 tsp	baking soda	5 mL
1 tsp	salt	5 mL
1 tsp	ground cinnamon	5 mL
1 tsp	ground ginger	5 mL
¼ tsp	ground nutmeg	1 mL
¼ tsp	anise seeds, crushed	1 mL
⅛ tsp	freshly ground black pepper	0.5 mL
½ cup	plain soy yogurt	125 mL
¼ cup	vegan margarine, melted	60 mL
2 tsp	finely grated orange zest	10 mL

1. In a medium saucepan, bring milk to a simmer over medium heat. Whisk in molasses and brown sugar, whisking, until sugar is dissolved. Transfer to a medium bowl and let cool.

2. Preheat oven to 325°F (160°C).

3. In a large bowl, whisk together all-purpose flour, rye flour, baking soda, salt, cinnamon, ginger, nutmeg, anise seeds and pepper.

4. Whisk yogurt, margarine and orange zest into the milk mixture until well blended.

5. Add the milk mixture to the flour mixture and stir until just blended.

6. Divide batter equally among prepared muffin cups.

7. Bake for 25 to 30 minutes or until a toothpick inserted in the center comes out clean. Let cool in pan on a wire rack for 5 minutes, then transfer to the rack to cool.

Gianduja Muffins (Switzerland)

Makes 12 muffins

The rich hazelnut-flavored chocolate called *gianduja* (or *gianduia* in Italy) — named for the masked character Gianduia of the centuries-old Italian *commedia dell'arte* — makes for a muffin that is sophisticated and intensely delicious.

- Preheat oven to 350°F (180°C)
- Food processor
- 12-cup muffin pan, greased

1 cup	chopped hazelnuts, toasted and cooled	250 mL
1 cup	vegan granulated sugar or evaporated cane juice, divided	250 mL
1½ cups	all-purpose flour	375 mL
⅔ cup	unsweetened cocoa powder (not Dutch process)	150 mL
1 tsp	baking powder	5 mL
1 tsp	baking soda	5 mL
½ tsp	salt	2 mL
½ cup	vegan margarine, softened	125 mL
1⅔ cups	plain soy yogurt	400 mL
1½ tsp	vanilla extract	7 mL
6 oz	vegan bittersweet chocolate, finely chopped	175 g

1. In food processor, process hazelnuts and ¼ cup (60 mL) of the sugar until finely chopped.

2. In a medium bowl, whisk together hazelnut mixture, flour, cocoa powder, baking powder, baking soda and salt.

3. In a large bowl, using an electric mixer on medium-high speed, beat the remaining sugar and margarine until light and fluffy. Beat in yogurt and vanilla until blended.

4. With the mixer on low speed, beat the flour mixture into the yogurt mixture until just blended. Using a rubber spatula, gently fold in chocolate.

5. Divide batter equally among prepared muffin cups.

6. Bake in preheated oven for 25 to 30 minutes or until tops are golden and a toothpick inserted in the center comes out clean. Let cool in pan on a wire rack for 5 minutes, then transfer to the rack to cool.

Piemontese Hazelnut, Chocolate and Orange Muffins (Italy)

Makes 12 muffins

This easy muffin draws inspiration from a divine Italian cake: *torta di nocciole*. The recipe for the cake was crafted by the extraordinary Lidia Bastianich, author and expert cook of all things Italian; I think she would approve of my muffin homage.

- Preheat oven to 400°F (200°C)
- 12-cup muffin pan, lined with paper liners

1¾ cups	all-purpose flour	425 mL
1 tsp	baking powder	5 mL
½ tsp	baking soda	2 mL
½ tsp	salt	2 mL
½ cup	vegan granulated sugar or evaporated cane juice	125 mL
¾ cup	plain soy yogurt	175 mL
½ cup	orange marmalade	125 mL
1 tsp	vanilla extract	5 mL
1 cup	chopped hazelnuts, toasted	250 mL
6 oz	vegan bittersweet chocolate, finely chopped	175 g

1. In a large bowl, whisk together flour, baking powder, baking soda and salt.

2. In a medium bowl, whisk together sugar, yogurt, marmalade and vanilla until well blended.

3. Add the yogurt mixture to the flour mixture and stir until just blended. Gently fold in hazelnuts and chocolate.

4. Divide batter equally among prepared muffin cups.

5. Bake in preheated oven for 18 to 23 minutes or until a toothpick inserted in the center comes out clean. Let cool in pan on a wire rack for 5 minutes, then transfer to the rack to cool.

Sachertorte Muffins (Austria)

Makes 12 muffins

I adore the flavor combination of chocolate and apricots that characterizes Sachertorte. The original is a refined, elegant ensemble, and these muffins follow suit. They are as at ease in a modern coffeehouse as in a 19th-century Viennese *kaffeehaus*.

Tip: Although apricot jam is the traditional choice for Sachertorte, you can use any other tart-sweet jams or preserves in its place. Try orange marmalade, raspberry jam or plum jam.

- Preheat oven to 400°F (200°C)
- 12-cup muffin pan, greased

2 cups	all-purpose flour	500 mL
1 cup	unsweetened cocoa powder (not Dutch process)	250 mL
1 tbsp	baking powder	15 mL
½ tsp	baking soda	2 mL
½ tsp	salt	2 mL
1 cup	vegan granulated sugar or evaporated cane juice	250 mL
1 cup	plain soy yogurt	250 mL
½ cup	non-dairy milk (soy, almond, rice, hemp)	125 mL
½ cup	vegan margarine, melted	125 mL
1 tsp	almond extract	5 mL
6 oz	vegan bittersweet chocolate, chopped	175 g
½ cup	apricot preserves	125 mL

1. In a large bowl, whisk together flour, cocoa powder, baking powder, baking soda and salt.

2. In a medium bowl, whisk together sugar, yogurt, milk, margarine and almond extract until well blended.

3. Add the yogurt mixture to the flour mixture and stir until just blended. Gently fold in chocolate.

4. Divide half the batter equally among prepared muffin cups. Spoon 2 tsp (10 mL) preserves into the center of each cup. Top with the remaining batter.

5. Bake in preheated oven for 21 to 25 minutes or until tops are firm to the touch. Let cool in pan on a wire rack for 5 minutes, then transfer to the rack to cool.

Mogyoró Muffins (Hungary)

Makes 12 muffins

Mogyoró — hazelnuts — are ubiquitous in Hungarian confections, from cookies to cakes to candies. Here, they star in an easily assembled muffin. A tender crumb, crunchy nuts and a tangy-sweet orange glaze add up to a muffin with Old World style.

> **Tip:** In addition to their rich, indulgent flavor, hazelnuts are one of the most nutritious nuts, providing vitamin E, dietary fiber, magnesium and heart-healthy B vitamins. Recent research shows that hazelnuts are also one of the highest natural sources of antioxidants.

- Preheat oven to 400°F (200°C)
- 12-cup muffin pan, lined with paper liners

Muffins

2 cups	all-purpose flour	500 mL
2 tsp	baking powder	10 mL
1 tsp	ground cinnamon	5 mL
¾ tsp	baking soda	3 mL
½ tsp	salt	2 mL
⅛ tsp	ground cloves	0.5 mL
¾ cup	vegan granulated sugar or evaporated cane juice	175 mL
½ cup	vegan margarine, softened	125 mL
½ cup	unsweetened applesauce	125 mL
2 tsp	finely grated orange zest	10 mL
1 tsp	vanilla extract	5 mL
½ cup	freshly squeezed orange juice	125 mL
1½ cups	chopped hazelnuts, toasted	375 mL

Glaze

1 cup	vegan confectioners' (icing) sugar	250 mL
2 tbsp	freshly squeezed orange juice	30 mL

1. *Muffins:* In a large bowl, whisk together flour, baking powder, cinnamon, baking soda, salt and cloves.

2. In a large bowl, using an electric mixer on medium-high speed, beat sugar and margarine until light and fluffy. Beat in applesauce until well blended. Beat in orange zest and vanilla until blended. Beat in orange juice until blended.

3. Add the flour mixture to the margarine mixture and, using a wooden spoon, stir until just blended. Gently fold in hazelnuts.

4. Divide batter equally among prepared muffin cups.

5. Bake in preheated oven for 18 to 21 minutes or until tops are golden and a toothpick inserted in the center comes out clean. Let cool in pan on a wire rack for 3 minutes, then transfer to the rack to cool.

6. *Glaze:* In a small bowl, whisk together confectioners' sugar and orange juice until blended. Spoon and spread over tops of cooled muffins.

Spiced Fig Muffins (Albania)

Makes 12 muffins

These muffins were developed for my dear friend Eralda, a beautiful, brilliant woman and fabulous cook who hails from Albania. We share a strong affection for figs (they are native to her homeland, Albania, and my home state, California), so I thought it fitting to develop a muffin based on an Albanian spiced, stewed fig recipe, *hoshaf me fiq të thatë*. In a word, they are heavenly.

Tips: If you have more citrus fruits on hand than you can use, grate or peel the zest, juice the fruit and freeze the zest and juice separately for up to 6 months.

Choose vacuum-packed dried figs for this recipe. They are typically shelved with raisins in the supermarket and are far softer than some of the hard-skinned options found in other sections of the store.

- Preheat oven to 350°F (180°C)
- 12-cup muffin pan, greased

2 1/2 cups	all-purpose flour	625 mL
2 1/4 tsp	baking powder	11 mL
3/4 tsp	baking soda	3 mL
1/2 tsp	salt	2 mL
1/2 tsp	ground cinnamon	2 mL
1/4 tsp	ground cloves	1 mL
1/8 tsp	freshly ground black pepper	0.5 mL
1 cup	packed vegan light brown sugar or Sucanat	250 mL
1/2 cup	olive oil or vegetable oil	125 mL
1 tbsp	finely grated lemon zest	15 mL
1 1/4 cups	vanilla-flavored or plain soy yogurt	300 mL
1 cup	chopped dried figs	250 mL

1. In a large bowl, whisk together flour, baking powder, baking soda, salt, cinnamon, cloves and pepper.

2. In a medium bowl, whisk together brown sugar, oil and lemon zest until well blended. Whisk in yogurt.

3. Add the yogurt mixture to the flour mixture and stir until just blended. Gently fold in figs.

4. Divide batter equally among prepared muffin cups.

5. Bake in preheated oven for 23 to 25 minutes or until tops are golden and a toothpick inserted in the center comes out clean. Let cool in pan on a wire rack for 5 minutes, then transfer to the rack to cool.

Rugalach Muffins (Eastern Europe)

Makes 18 muffins

Popular throughout Eastern Europe, rugalach are rolled triangles of tender pastry encasing a not-too-sweet fruit, nut and spice filling. I've captured the same flavors here: each muffin boasts a rich, velvety batter layered with walnuts, raisins and cinnamon, imbued with the floral notes of vanilla and finished with a surprise of apricot preserves.

> **Tip:** Sprinkle a little flour over the dried fruit before and after you chop it. The first dusting keeps the fruit from sticking to the knife; the second coats the individual pieces and keeps them separated during mixing.

- Preheat oven to 350°F (180°C)
- Two 12-cup muffin pans, 18 cups lined with paper liners

2 cups	all-purpose flour	500 mL
2½ tsp	baking powder	12 mL
½ tsp	salt	2 mL
1½ cups	vegan granulated sugar or evaporated cane juice, divided	375 mL
8 oz	non-dairy cream cheese (such as Tofutti brand), softened	250 g
1 cup	vegan margarine, softened	250 mL
1 tsp	vanilla extract	5 mL
¾ cup	unsweetened applesauce	175 mL
½ cup	golden raisins, chopped	125 mL
½ cup	finely chopped walnuts, toasted	125 mL
1 tsp	ground cinnamon	5 mL
¼ cup	apricot preserves	60 mL

1. In a medium bowl, whisk together flour, baking powder and salt.

2. In a large bowl, using an electric mixer on medium-high speed, beat 1¼ cups (300 mL) of the sugar, cream cheese, margarine and vanilla until light and fluffy. Beat in applesauce until well blended.

3. With the mixer on low speed, beat the flour mixture into the applesauce mixture until just blended.

4. In a small bowl, combine the remaining sugar, raisins, walnuts and cinnamon.

5. Divide half the batter equally among prepared muffin cups. Spoon 1 tsp (5 mL) preserves and 1 tbsp (15 mL) raisin mixture into the center of each cup. Top with the remaining batter.

6. Bake in preheated oven for 25 to 30 minutes or until tops are golden and firm to the touch. Let cool in pans on a wire rack for 5 minutes, then transfer to the rack to cool.

Black Bread Muffins (Russia)

Makes 12 muffins

No staple is as important to a Russian table as bread; it even has its own laws, regulations and price controls. In times of plenty and celebration, Russian black bread, rich with wheat, rye, coffee, molasses, fennel and caraway, is made and eaten as a symbol of wealth and health. But you can make these muffins for any occasion.

Tip: Cocoa powder contributes to the dark complexion and overall nutrition of these easy muffins. Cocoa contains polyphenols (similar to those found in wine) with antioxidant compounds (called flavonoids) that may reduce blood pressure and benefit heart function.

- Preheat oven to 375°F (190°C)
- 12-cup muffin pan, greased

1¼ cups	non-dairy milk (soy, almond, rice, hemp)	300 mL
1½ tbsp	cider vinegar	22 mL
1 cup	rye flour	250 mL
1 cup	all-purpose flour	250 mL
⅓ cup	natural bran	75 mL
2 tbsp	unsweetened cocoa powder (not Dutch process)	30 mL
2 tsp	baking powder	10 mL
1 tsp	baking soda	5 mL
1 tsp	salt	5 mL
¾ tsp	fennel seeds, crushed	3 mL
½ tsp	caraway seeds, crushed	2 mL
2 tsp	instant espresso powder	10 mL
¼ cup	dark (cooking) molasses	60 mL
¼ cup	vegan margarine, melted	60 mL

1. In a glass measuring cup, combine milk and vinegar. Let stand for 5 minutes.

2. In a large bowl, whisk together rye flour, all-purpose flour, bran, cocoa powder, baking powder, baking soda, salt, fennel seeds and caraway seeds.

3. In a medium bowl, whisk together espresso powder, molasses and margarine until well blended. Whisk in milk mixture until blended.

4. Add the milk mixture to the flour mixture and stir until just blended.

5. Divide batter equally among prepared muffin cups.

6. Bake in preheated oven for 20 to 25 minutes or until a toothpick inserted in the center comes out clean. Let cool in pan on a wire rack for 5 minutes, then transfer to the rack to cool.

Couscous Date Muffins (Morocco)

Makes 12 muffins

Couscous and dates are staples of the Moroccan table. Both are used in savory dishes but also star in a variety of simple desserts. These muffins showcase both ingredients with panache. Orange marmalade adds extra flavor.

> **Tip:** Many people think of couscous as a grain, but it is actually a North African pasta (small grains of semolina coated in wheat flour). For additional nutty flavor — and whole-grain nutrition — use whole wheat couscous in place of regular couscous.

- 12-cup muffin pan, lined with paper liners

1 cup	couscous	250 mL
1 cup	boiling water	250 mL
1¾ cups	all-purpose flour	425 mL
1 tsp	baking powder	5 mL
½ tsp	baking soda	2 mL
½ tsp	salt	2 mL
½ cup	packed vegan light brown sugar or Sucanat	125 mL
¾ cup	plain soy yogurt	125 mL
½ cup	orange marmalade	125 mL
1 cup	pitted dates, chopped	250 mL

1. In a small bowl, combine couscous and boiling water. Cover with a plate and let stand for 5 minutes. Uncover and fluff with a fork. Let cool to room temperature.

2. Preheat oven to 400°F (200°C).

3. In a large bowl, whisk together flour, baking powder, baking soda and salt.

4. In a medium bowl, whisk together sugar, yogurt and marmalade until well blended.

5. Add the yogurt mixture to the flour mixture and stir until just blended. Gently fold in couscous and dates.

6. Divide batter evenly among prepared muffin cups.

7. Bake for 17 to 22 minutes or until a toothpick inserted in the center comes out clean. Let cool in pan on a wire rack for 5 minutes, then transfer to the rack to cool.

Orange Flower Water Muffins
(Algeria)

Makes 12 muffins

A perfumed distillation of bitter orange blossoms, orange flower water is used in many North African sweets. It has a delicate, floral taste and fragrance that works especially well with citrus and the subtle floral notes of agave nectar.

Tips: Look for orange flower water at liquor stores and in the international or specialty foods sections of some supermarkets.

An equal amount of chopped dried apricots may be used in place of the golden raisins.

- Preheat oven to 350°F (180°C)
- 12-cup muffin pan, greased

2 1/2 cups	all-purpose flour	625 mL
2 1/2 tsp	baking powder	12 mL
1/2 tsp	salt	2 mL
1 cup	agave nectar	250 mL
1 cup	non-dairy milk (soy, almond, rice, hemp)	250 mL
1/2 cup	olive oil	125 mL
1 tbsp	finely grated orange zest	15 mL
1 1/2 tsp	orange flower water	7 mL
2/3 cup	golden raisins, chopped	150 mL

1. In a large bowl, whisk together flour, baking powder and salt.

2. In a medium bowl, whisk together agave nectar, milk, oil, orange zest and orange flower water until well blended.

3. Add the milk mixture to the flour mixture and stir until just blended. Gently fold in raisins.

4. Divide batter equally among prepared muffin cups.

5. Bake in preheated oven for 23 to 25 minutes or until tops are golden and a toothpick inserted in the center comes out clean. Let cool in pan on a wire rack for 5 minutes, then transfer to the rack to cool.

Turkish Coffee Muffins (Turkey)

Makes 12 muffins

Turkish coffee is prepared by boiling finely powdered roasted coffee beans in a pot called a *cezve*, along with sugar and cardamom. It is then served in a small cup, where the dregs settle. The same marriage of cardamom and dark coffee is exceptional in these muffins.

> **Tip:** For caffeine-free muffins, use 1/4 cup (60 mL) instant decaffeinated coffee powder in place of the espresso powder.

- Preheat oven to 350°F (180°C)
- 12-cup muffin pan, lined with paper liners

2 cups	all-purpose flour	500 mL
1 1/4 tsp	ground cardamom	6 mL
1 1/4 tsp	baking soda	6 mL
1/4 tsp	salt	1 mL
2/3 cup	warm water	150 mL
2 tbsp	instant espresso powder	30 mL
3/4 cup	vegan granulated sugar or evaporated cane juice	175 mL
1/2 cup	plain soy yogurt	125 mL
1/2 cup	dark (cooking) molasses	125 mL
1/3 cup	vegetable oil	75 mL
2 tbsp	vegan confectioners' (icing) sugar	30 mL

1. In a large bowl, whisk together flour, cardamom, baking soda and salt.

2. In a small bowl or glass measuring cup, whisk together warm water and espresso powder until espresso powder is dissolved.

3. In a medium bowl, whisk together granulated sugar, yogurt, molasses and oil until smooth. Whisk in espresso mixture until blended.

4. Add the espresso mixture to the flour mixture and stir until just blended.

5. Divide batter equally among prepared muffin cups.

6. Bake in preheated oven for 24 to 27 minutes or until a toothpick inserted in the center comes out clean. Let cool in pan on a wire rack for 3 minutes, then transfer to the rack to cool. Dust cooled muffin tops with confectioners' sugar.

Tabbouleh Muffins (Lebanon, Israel, Syria)

Makes 12 muffins

Tabbouleh is quintessential Middle Eastern fare, a delectable combination of bulgur (cracked wheat), tomatoes, fresh herbs and lemon. A short while back, it dawned on me that I could reinterpret this favorite salad into a portable muffin. I think you'll love the result as much as I do.

> **Tips:** You can use the oil from the tomatoes to make up some of the oil needed for the muffin batter.
>
> Chop fresh mint with your sharpest knife. Like many herbs, mint bruises easily and, when bruised, it loses its volatile, flavorful oils. To keep bruising to a minimum, use a sharp, dry knife for chopping and slicing.

- 12-cup muffin pan, greased

¹⁄₂ cup	bulgur	125 mL
1 cup	boiling water	250 mL
1²⁄₃ cups	whole wheat pastry flour	400 mL
2¹⁄₂ tsp	baking powder	12 mL
1¹⁄₄ tsp	salt	6 mL
³⁄₄ tsp	baking soda	3 mL
1 tbsp	vegan granulated sugar or evaporated cane juice	15 mL
1 cup	non-dairy milk (soy, almond, rice, hemp)	250 mL
¹⁄₂ cup	olive oil or vegetable oil	125 mL
1 tbsp	finely grated lemon zest	15 mL
2 tbsp	freshly squeezed lemon juice	30 mL
¹⁄₂ cup	chopped green onions (scallions)	125 mL
¹⁄₂ cup	loosely packed fresh mint leaves, chopped	125 mL
¹⁄₂ cup	chopped drained oil-packed sun-dried tomatoes	125 mL

1. In a small bowl, combine bulgur and boiling water. Let stand for 30 minutes. Drain off any excess water.

2. Preheat oven to 425°F (220°C).

3. In a large bowl, whisk together flour, baking powder, salt and baking soda.

4. In a medium bowl, whisk together sugar, milk, oil, lemon zest and lemon juice until well blended.

5. Add the milk mixture to the flour mixture and stir until just blended. Gently stir in bulgur, green onions, mint and tomatoes.

6. Divide batter equally among prepared muffin cups.

7. Bake for 16 to 20 minutes or until tops are golden brown and a toothpick inserted in the center comes out clean. Let cool in pan on a wire rack for 5 minutes, then transfer to the rack to cool slightly. Serve warm or let cool completely.

Sweet Tahini Muffins (Israel)

Makes 18 muffins

Tahini is just as delicious — I would argue even more so — in sweets as it is in hummus and baba ghanouj. Halvah, a delicious, fudge-like candy made from tahini, is one such beloved sweet. These muffins may soon become another.

- Preheat oven to 350°F (180°C)
- Two 12-cup muffin pans, 18 cups greased

Muffins

1 1/3 cups	non-dairy milk (soy, almond, rice, hemp)	325 mL
1 1/2 tbsp	cider vinegar	22 mL
2 cups	quick-cooking rolled oats	500 mL
1 cup	all-purpose flour	250 mL
1/2 cup	whole wheat flour	125 mL
2 tsp	baking powder	10 mL
1/2 tsp	baking soda	2 mL
1/2 tsp	salt	2 mL
1 cup	packed vegan light brown sugar or Sucanat	250 mL
1/2 cup	tahini, well-stirred	125 mL
1/2 cup	coconut oil, warmed, or vegetable oil	125 mL
1 tsp	vanilla extract	5 mL
1/2 cup	finely chopped walnuts, toasted	125 mL

Glaze

1/3 cup	tahini, well-stirred	75 mL
2 tbsp	non-dairy milk (soy, almond, rice, hemp)	30 mL
1 tsp	vanilla extract	5 mL
1 cup	vegan confectioners' (icing) sugar	250 mL

1. *Muffins:* In a glass measuring cup, combine milk and vinegar. Let stand for 5 minutes.

2. In a large bowl, whisk together oats, all-purpose flour, whole wheat flour, baking powder, baking soda and salt.

3. In a medium bowl, whisk together brown sugar, tahini, coconut oil and vanilla until well blended. Whisk in milk mixture until blended.

Tip: Tahini is a thick paste made from ground sesame seeds and is used predominantly in Middle Eastern dishes such as hummus. Because the seeds are ground to a paste, tahini is very easy to digest, and many of its nutrients — notably B vitamins and calcium — find their way into the bloodstream within about half an hour of consumption.

4. Add the milk mixture to the flour mixture and stir until just blended. Gently fold in walnuts.

5. Divide batter equally among prepared muffin cups.

6. Bake in preheated oven for 22 to 27 minutes or until tops are golden brown and a toothpick inserted in the center comes out clean. Let cool in pans on a wire rack for 5 minutes, then transfer to the rack to cool.

7. *Glaze:* In a small bowl, whisk together tahini, milk and vanilla until blended. Whisk in confectioners' sugar until blended and smooth. Spoon over tops of cooled muffins.

Rose Water Muffins
(Iraq, Iran, Turkey and India)

Makes 12 muffins

These easily assembled, exotic muffins, with a drizzle of rose-scented icing and a cardamom-infused batter, are inspired by the aromatics found in Persian, Turkish and Indian confections.

Tip: Rose water is a by-product of the production of rose oil. When rose petals and water are distilled, the leftover liquid is used as rose water. It is used in a variety of Middle Eastern dishes. Look for it in Middle Eastern grocery stores, well-stocked supermarkets (either in the ethnic foods section or the baking aisle), gourmet grocers and health food stores.

• Preheat oven to 400°F (200°C)
• 12-cup muffin pan, greased

Muffins

2¼ cups	all-purpose flour	550 mL
1 tbsp	baking powder	15 mL
½ tsp	baking soda	2 mL
½ tsp	salt	2 mL
½ tsp	ground cardamom	2 mL
¾ cup	vegan granulated sugar or evaporated cane juice	175 mL
⅓ cup	coconut oil, warmed, or vegan margarine, melted	75 mL
1 tsp	rose water	5 mL
1⅓ cups	plain soy yogurt	325 mL
½ cup	non-dairy milk (soy, almond, rice, hemp)	125 L

Icing

1 cup	vegan confectioners' (icing) sugar	250 mL
2 tbsp	non-dairy milk (soy, almond, rice, hemp)	30 mL
¼ tsp	rose water	1 mL

1. *Muffins:* In a large bowl, whisk together flour, baking powder, baking soda, salt and cardamom.

2. In a medium bowl, whisk together sugar, coconut oil and rose water until well blended. Whisk in yogurt and milk until blended.

3. Add the yogurt mixture to the flour mixture and stir until just blended.

4. Divide batter equally among prepared muffin cups.

5. Bake in preheated oven for 21 to 26 minutes or until tops are golden and firm to the touch. Let cool in pan on a wire rack for 5 minutes, then transfer to the rack to cool.

6. *Icing:* In a small bowl, whisk together confectioners' sugar, milk and rose water until blended and smooth. Drizzle over tops of cooled muffins.

Gajar Halvah Muffins (India)

Makes 18 muffins

Gajar halvah, a luxurious Indian dessert made from carrots slowly cooked down with sweetened milk and spices, is the inspiration for these muffins. This riff is fast enough for any day of the week and makes for an amazing start to the day.

Tip: Don't peel carrots if they're young and tender; the skin packs a lot of flavor, as well as vitamins. As carrots mature, though, their skin becomes a little bitter, so go ahead and peel it off with a vegetable peeler.

- Preheat oven to 350°F (180°C)
- Two 12-cup muffin pans, 18 cups greased

1²⁄₃ cups	all-purpose flour	400 mL
1¹⁄₂ tsp	baking powder	7 mL
1 tsp	ground cardamom	5 mL
¹⁄₂ tsp	baking soda	2 mL
¹⁄₂ tsp	salt	2 mL
1 cup	packed vegan light brown sugar or Sucanat	250 mL
³⁄₄ cup	plain soy yogurt	175 mL
¹⁄₂ cup	coconut oil, warmed, or vegan margarine, melted	125 mL
1 tbsp	finely grated orange zest	15 mL
3 cups	finely shredded carrots	750 mL
²⁄₃ cup	golden raisins, chopped	150 mL
¹⁄₂ cup	chopped pistachios	125 mL

1. In a large bowl, whisk together flour, baking powder, cardamom, baking soda and salt.

2. In a medium bowl, whisk together brown sugar, yogurt, coconut oil and orange zest until blended.

3. Add the yogurt mixture to the flour mixture and stir until just blended. Gently fold in carrots and raisins.

4. Divide batter equally among prepared muffin cups. Sprinkle with pistachios.

5. Bake in preheated oven for 20 to 25 minutes or until tops are golden and a toothpick inserted in the center comes out clean. Let cool in pans on a wire rack for 5 minutes, then transfer to the rack to cool.

Star Anise and Pineapple Muffins (Malaysia)

Makes 12 muffins

Licorice-like star anise is a common spice in Malay cooking, used in both sweet and savory dishes. It perfumes these lush, fragrant, tropical muffins, complementing the bright notes of another Malaysian favorite, pineapple.

Tip: Star anise is a small, dark brown fruit that comes from a petite evergreen tree or bush. As the name suggests, it is star-shaped, with a mahogany-colored pea-sized seed in each of its eight segments. It is harvested just before it ripens and is always used dried. It has a very strong licorice-like flavor and aroma and is used in a variety of Asian dishes. Look for it at Asian grocery stores and well-stocked supermarkets. In a pinch, you can crush an equal amount of anise seeds or fennel seeds as a substitute.

- Preheat oven to 400°F (200°C)
- 12-cup muffin pan, greased

1	can (15 oz/425 mL) pineapple tidbits	1
2¾ cups	all-purpose flour	675 mL
1 tbsp	baking powder	15 mL
½ tsp	baking soda	2 mL
½ tsp	salt	2 mL
½ tsp	ground star anise	2 mL
¾ cup	packed vegan light brown sugar or Sucanat	175 mL
½ cup	coconut oil, warmed, or vegetable oil	125 mL
½ cup	plain soy yogurt	125 mL
1 tbsp	finely grated lime zest	15 mL

1. Drain juice from pineapple tidbits into a glass measuring cup. Pat tidbits dry and set aside. Add enough water to juice in measuring cup to make 1 cup (250 mL). Set aside.

2. In a large bowl, whisk together flour, baking powder, baking soda, salt and star anise.

3. In a medium bowl, whisk together brown sugar, coconut oil, yogurt and lime zest until blended. Whisk in pineapple juice mixture until just blended.

4. Add the yogurt mixture to the flour mixture and stir until just blended. Gently fold in pineapple tidbits.

5. Divide batter equally among prepared muffin cups.

6. Bake in preheated oven for 20 to 25 minutes or until tops are golden and a toothpick inserted in the center comes out clean. Let cool in pan on a wire rack for 5 minutes, then transfer to the rack to cool.

Sesame Ginger Muffins (China)

Makes 12 muffins

The traditional Chinese combination of sesame and ginger is one of the best flavor duets around. Here, it is showcased in non-traditional but addictively delicious muffin form.

> **Tip:** Sesame, in all its forms (whole seeds, oil and paste), is packed with nutrients, including vitamin E and calcium.

- Preheat oven to 375°F (190°C)
- 12-cup muffin pan, lined with paper liners

2 cups	all-purpose flour	500 mL
1/4 cup	sesame seeds	60 mL
2 1/2 tsp	baking powder	12 mL
2 1/2 tsp	ground ginger	12 mL
1/2 tsp	salt	2 mL
2/3 cup	packed vegan light brown sugar or Sucanat	150 mL
1/4 cup	vegetable oil	60 mL
1 tbsp	toasted sesame oil	15 mL
1/2 tsp	almond extract	2 mL
1 cup	vanilla-flavored soy yogurt	250 mL

1. In a large bowl, whisk together flour, sesame seeds, baking powder, ginger and salt.

2. In a medium bowl, whisk together brown sugar, vegetable oil, sesame oil and almond extract until well blended. Whisk in yogurt.

3. Add the yogurt mixture to the flour mixture and stir until just blended.

4. Divide batter equally among prepared muffin cups.

5. Bake in preheated oven for 18 to 21 minutes or until tops are golden and a toothpick inserted in the center comes out clean. Let cool in pan on a wire rack for 5 minutes, then transfer to the rack to cool.

Five-Spice Asian Pear Muffins (China)

Makes 12 muffins

These not-too-sweet muffins are moist, tender and innovative, but not remotely fussy.

- Preheat oven to 400°F (200°C)
- 12-cup muffin pan, greased

1 ½ cups	all-purpose flour	375 mL
½ cup	whole wheat flour	125 mL
2 tsp	baking powder	10 mL
1 ¼ tsp	Chinese five-spice powder	6 mL
½ tsp	baking soda	2 mL
½ tsp	salt	2 mL
½ cup	vegan granulated sugar or evaporated cane juice	125 mL
1 cup	plain soy yogurt	250 mL
½ cup	unsweetened apple juice	125 mL
⅓ cup	vegetable oil	75 mL
1 tsp	vanilla extract	5 mL
1 ½ cups	chopped peeled Asian pears	375 mL

1. In a large bowl, whisk together all-purpose flour, whole wheat flour, baking powder, five-spice powder, baking soda and salt.

2. In a medium bowl, whisk together sugar, yogurt, apple juice, oil and vanilla until well blended.

3. Add the yogurt mixture to the flour mixture and stir until just blended. Gently fold in pears.

4. Divide batter equally among prepared muffin cups.

5. Bake in preheated oven for 20 to 25 minutes or until tops are golden brown and a toothpick inserted in the center comes out clean. Let cool in pan on a wire rack for 3 minutes, then transfer to the rack to cool.

Library and Archives Canada Cataloguing in Publication

Saulsbury, Camilla V.
    150 best vegan muffin recipes / Camilla V. Saulsbury.

Includes index.
ISBN 978-0-7788-0292-1

    1. Muffins. 2. Vegan cooking. 3. Cookbooks. I. Title.
II. Title: One hundred fifty best vegan muffin recipes.

TX770.M83S375 2012   641.81'57   C2011-907397-8

Index

Whole Wheat Blackberry Crumb
Muffins, 46
Wild Rice Hazelnut Muffins, 144
flour, whole wheat. *See* whole wheat
flour
flours, 9–10. *See also specific types of flour*
measuring, 10
French Toast Muffins, 84
fruit, 19. *See also* berries; jams and
preserves; *specific fruits*
Fresh Plum Muffins with Walnut
Sugar Tops, 90
Fruit, Flax and Oat Muffins, 62
Georgia Peach Muffins, 53
Mango Muffins with Cardamom
Crumble, 96
Muesli Muffins, 81
Persimmon Muffins, 61
Pineapple Lime Muffins, 60
Rhubarb Muffins, 68
Trail Mix Muffins, 67
Tropical Fruit Muffins with Coconut
Streusel, 94

G

Gajar Halvah Muffins, 179
Georgia Peach Muffins, 53
Gianduja Muffins, 165
ginger
Candied Ginger Muffins, 106
Gingerbread Muffins, 40
Sesame Ginger Muffins, 181
granola cereal
Granola Dried Blueberry Muffins, 48
Trail Mix Muffins, 67
Green Olive Muffins, 161
Green Onion Muffins, 129
Guinness Muffins, 154

H

hazelnuts
Cherry Hazelnut Muffins, 89
Gianduja Muffins, 165
Mogyoró Muffins, 168
Piemontese Hazelnut, Chocolate and
Orange Muffins, 166
Wild Rice Hazelnut Muffins, 144

hemp milk, 16
herbs. *See also specific herbs*
Corn Muffins, Tried and True
(variation), 35
Fresh Herb Muffins, 37
Herbed Rye Muffins, 119
Parsley Lemon Muffins, 124
Sweet Potato Sage Muffins, 142
Tabbouleh Muffins, 175
Whole Wheat Walnut Muffins
(variation), 72
honey, 14

I

ingredients, 9–19
measuring, 8, 10
organic, 19
Irish Brown Bread Muffins, 117

J

Jalapeño Corn Muffins, 123
jams and preserves
Berry Jam Muffins, 25
Couscous Date Muffins, 172
Jelly Doughnut Muffins, 97
Peanut Butter and Jelly Muffins, 105
Piemontese Hazelnut, Chocolate and
Orange Muffins, 166
Raspberry Trifle Muffins, 158
Rugalach Muffins, 170
Sachertorte Muffins, 167
jumbo muffins, 7

K

Kale and Toasted Walnut Muffins, 126
Kasha Muffins, 77

L

leaveners, 11–12
lemon
Blueberry Lemon Muffins, 47
Dried Cherry Corn Muffins, 51
Lemon Berry Corn Muffins, 54
Lemon Polenta Muffins, 91
Lemon Poppy Seed Muffins, 28
Muhammara Muffins, 135